BOOK OF BLACK HEROES

POLITICAL LEADERS PAST AND PRESENT

An Introduction to Important Black Achievers

BY GIL L. ROBERTSON IV

Published by Just Us Books, Inc. P.O. Box 5306, East Orange, NJ 07019

HTTP://justusbooks.com
ISBN: 978-1-933491-21-9
e-ISBN: 978-1-933491-22-6
Printed in the USA
10 9 8 7 6 5 4 3 2 1

CONTENTS

STATE LEADERS

MUNICIPAL LEADERS

Foreword

The United States of America, as well as the rest of our world, is faced with many challenges. We observe from afar—starving and ill children without proper healthcare, improper housing, limited education needed to enable one to prosper in a highly technological world, a global economy unable to sustain itself, a warming climate and oil spills that threaten our wildlife, and the loss of many jobs.

All of these issues may seem negative—yet, there is always a hopeful today and future. Since the first recording of human existence, men and women have met all of the challenges of life with resolve to find answers that will benefit everyone.

These people are called "leaders." Some are known; most are not. These are our next-door neighbors, friends, teachers, some politicians, business executives, and volunteers in our community. These people are leaders who have the ability to unite others around an idea—a concept needed to find solutions.

There are different kinds of leaders. One group declares themselves "the leaders" while only looking for self-gratification and praise. Another group motivates the masses around a common cause, and they use their skills to organize effectively to achieve change for the good of all people. Dr. Martin Luther King, Jr., was such a leader. So was Medgar Evers, a civil rights leader in Mississippi (1953–1963) who was assassinated for his successful leadership in motivating people to register and vote and to eliminate discrimination in all areas of American life.

The third group encompasses the reluctant leaders. Due to unplanned circumstances, they are forced into that role. I am such an example. The public deemed me a leader after my husband, Medgar, was assassinated. Perhaps I am best known for my work as the chairperson of the civil rights organization the National Association for the Advancement of Colored People (NAACP)—the largest civil rights organization in the world.

Today, your generation has the ability to achieve your highest goals through good educational opportunities and to be inspired by those of my generation who paid a tremendous price for the freedoms you now enjoy.

You have the responsibility to "be the best" in whatever goals you pursue. You are the leaders of today and the future.

—Mrs. Myrlie Evers-Williams

LEADERSHIP

noun

The action of leading a group of people or an organization.
"different styles of leadership"

synonyms: guidance, direction, control, management,
superintendence, supervision; organization,
government
"firm leadership"

• The state or position of being a leader.
"the leadership of the party"

synonyms: directorship, governorship, governance,
administration, captaincy, control, ascendancy,
supremacy, rule, command, power, dominion,
influence
"the leadership of the Coalition"

• The leaders of an organization, country, etc.
plural noun: leaderships
"a change of leadership had become desirable"

Source: https://www.google.com/#q=Leadership

Introduction

When I was a young boy, the one thing that all of my friends and I wanted to be was a leader. At the time, of course, none of us knew what a leader really was. All we knew was that they were cool and popular in our community, something that we wanted to be.

Now it takes more than being cool and popular to become a good leader. Being a leader is a tough job that requires a lot of discipline, intelligence, and wisdom. Although some people are natural born leaders, most have to be taught. A good leader assumes the responsibility for inspiring and managing others and showing them the best ways to achieve a goal or objective. Leadership also means sometimes sacrificing one's own ego so that others are allowed to participate.

In ways large and small, leaders help to shape and influence the lives of others. They are found at every level of society, and they include some of the people with whom we interact daily. They are parents, siblings, teachers, religious leaders, doctors, coaches, school bus drivers, and police officers.

Some people have demonstrated an ability to lead large groups of people or to fight for an important cause. They are chosen because of their skills and the faith that their supporters have in them. Political leaders are a part of this group. Throughout American history, there have been countless numbers of men and women who have helped to lay the foundation for our democratic form of government. Included among them is a long list of African Americans.

The first African-American political leaders began to serve following the American Civil War and the end of slavery. To be accepted back into the Union, the federal government set up laws and conditions that the southern states had to follow, including ensuring the rights of newly freed African Americans. Federal troops were employed throughout the South to enforce these laws and conditions. Known as Reconstruction, this period represented a window of opportunity for African Americans in all areas of life. Many African-American political leaders emerged during this period, using their political power and influence to push for equality and justice for all Americans. They held local, state, and national offices, and they served as judges and law enforcement officials.

Unfortunately, the Reconstruction period was short-lived, lasting only from 1865 to 1877. States in the South as well as states in other parts of the country then passed laws that essentially took away the citizenship rights of African Americans, including the right to vote and hold elected office. These legislative measures were called *Jim Crow laws*.

It would take nearly 100 years and the gains of the Civil Rights Movement before African Americans would again be guaranteed the right to vote and hold political office. A new group of political leaders symbolized the dramatic changes that took place in the United States during the 1950s and 1960s. These political leaders were emblematic of the country's move, however slow, to live up to its founding principles. The political leaders who emerged during this period, the 1950s and 1960s, symbolized the dramatic changes that took place in the United States.

A new generation of Black political leaders is active today. These leaders carry on the legacy of those who came before them, working to protect the civil and human rights of all Americans.

Book of Black Heroes: Political Leaders Past and Present will acquaint readers with political leaders of the past, and will introduce new leaders who are presently making their mark in the world of politics. Through their stories, I hope others, especially young people, will be inspired to become leaders in their own right.

— Gil L. Robertson IV

PRESIDENT

"Progress does not compel us to settle centuries-long debates about the role of government for all time, but it does require us to act in our time."

—President Barack Obama
from his Second Inaugural Address, 2013

OBARA, BARACK H.

FORTY-FOURTH PRESIDENT OF THE UNITED STATES

1961

"Change will not come if we wait for some other person or some other time. We are the ones we've been waiting for. We are the change that we seek."

Barack Obama's election as the forty-fourth president of the United States represented a seismic shift in the history of the United States. Elected for his first term in office in 2008 (146 years after the Emancipation Proclamation freed Blacks from slavery), Obama's ascent to the nation's highest political office symbolized a turn in American politics that some previously thought impossible. His reelection in 2012 further signaled a change in the attitudes toward people of African descent in leadership positions.

Born in Honolulu, Hawaii, in 1961 to a father from Kenya and a mother from Kansas City, Missouri, Obama is the first U.S. president born in America's fiftieth state. Raised by his mom and grandparents in locales both in the United States and Asia, the young Obama experienced a variety of cultures in a climate of mutual respect.

After graduating from high school, Obama moved to Los Angeles where he attended Occidental College. It was there that he began his career as a political advocate by calling for the college to disinvest from South Africa due to apartheid. For his junior year, he transferred to Columbia University in New York City where he earned a BA degree in political science. He then worked in the business sector for two years before moving to Chicago where he became a community organizer working on behalf of low-income residents.

Obama next entered Harvard Law School. At the end of his first year he was selected as an editor of the prestigious *Harvard Law Review*. The following year he went a step further by being named the publication's president, and earned the opportunity to serve as research assistant to the constitutional scholar Laurence Tribe. Obama graduated *magna cum laude* from Harvard in 1991 and returned to Chicago where he practiced civil rights law and organized voter registration drives.

Helping to make a difference in the lives of others inspired Obama to run for a seat in the Illinois State Senate where he could help pass laws to help his constituents. He won the Democratic primary unopposed and went on to carry the general election with more than 82 percent of the vote. During his first years as a state senator, Obama co-sponsored a bill that restructured the Illinois welfare program. He also helped get passed various pieces of legislation that established a tax credit for working families, increased child care subsidies for low-income families, and expanded healthcare services and early childhood education programs for the poor.

After an unsuccessful primary run for a seat in the U.S. House of Representatives, Obama turned his sights toward the U.S. Senate. Mounting a highly organized and well-financed campaign, he swept the highly competitive Democratic primary, before a general election contest against Republican candidate

Jack Ryan. When Ryan had to pull out of the campaign, former diplomat Alan Keyes replaced him in the race. Although Keyes was also Black and equally well financed, Obama prevailed in the race, earning the largest margin of victory in the history of an Illinois U.S. Senate contest. With his win, Obama became only the third African American elected to the U.S. Senate since Reconstruction.

As senator, Obama took part in bipartisan efforts to improve border security and immigration reform. He also partnered with his Republican colleagues on a bill that expanded efforts to destroy weapons of mass destruction. After Hurricane Katrina, Obama also spoke out for victims of that natural disaster and pushed for alternative energy development and improved veterans' benefits. He held numerous assignments on Senate Committees for Foreign Relations; Health, Education, Labor, and Pensions; Homeland Security and Governmental Affairs; and Veterans' Affairs. He was a member of the Congressional Black Caucus, and a chairperson of the Subcommittee on European Affairs.

In February 2007, Obama made international headlines when he announced his candidacy for the 2008 Democratic presidential nomination. He ran a tight battle with former first lady and then–U.S. senator from New York, Hillary Rodham Clinton. After winning the required number of delegates to earn the Democratic nomination, Obama then mounted a general election campaign against Republican presidential nominee John McCain. The resulting contest was often controversial, expensive, and hard fought, but Obama prevailed, winning the election as the forty-fourth president of the United States and the first African American to hold this office.

When Obama took office, he faced a number of obstacles and scored some victories as well. With the country in a deep economic recession, two ongoing foreign wars, and other social and political problems, he took action on many fronts. During his first 100 days in office, he convinced Congress to expand healthcare insurance for children and provide legal protection for women seeking equal pay. He also successfully pushed through Congress a stimulus bill to promote short-term economic growth. Most notable during his first term in office, Obama signed into law his healthcare reform plan, known as the Affordable Care Act, which provided medical care access to millions of Americans. He later signed a repeal of the military policy known as "Don't Ask, Don't Tell," which prevented openly gay people from serving in the U.S. Armed Forces. In foreign affairs, he reached out to improve relations with Europe, China, and Russia and to open dialogue with Iran, Venezuela, and Cuba. The Nobel Committee in Norway recognized Obama's push for peace and diplomacy by awarding him the 2009 Nobel Peace Prize.

In November 2012, President Obama defeated Mitt Romney, the Republican nominee, to win a second term.

During his two terms in office, Obama has realized many of the ambitious goals that he set out to achieve when he was first elected. Addressing financial reform, alternative energy, education reform, healthcare insurance coverage for more Americans—all the while bringing down the national debt, he has led the nation through many difficult challenges. Although history will be the final judge of Obama's time in office, his record speaks of a leader who has steered America in the right direction.

GOVERNORS

"We mark today not a victory party or the accomplishments of an individual but the triumph of an idea, an idea as old as America, as old as the God who looks out for us all."

—The Honorable L. Douglas Wilder
from his Inaugural Address as Governor
January 13, 1990, Richmond, Virginia

PATERSON, DAVID

GOVERNOR OF NEW YORK

1954

"Always believe in yourself."

Born the son of longtime New York State and Harlem political leader Basil A. Paterson, David Paterson would go on to surpass even his father's notable accomplishments. Paterson would become the first African-American governor in the history of New York State.

Although he was born legally blind, Paterson attended regular classes in school where he was well liked, and he performed well academically. But his disability was not without challenges.

"It was very important to my parents and me that I learn how to live in mainstream society," he said. "I never studied Braille or used a cane or seeing-eye dog. I just dug in deep, determined to be the best that I could be."

Paterson adjusted well throughout his grade school years, and he graduated early from high school. However, the new obstacles that he faced in college nearly caused him to flunk out.

"College life for me was a big challenge at first," he recalled. "It was a totally different environment, and I had trouble managing the expectations. So I decided to take a year off to learn how to adapt to my new adult life."

After moving into the workforce, Paterson regained his confidence and returned to his college studies. He earned an undergraduate degree from Columbia University in 1977 and a law degree from Hofstra University Law School in 1982. After working for the Queens District Attorney's office, he joined the staff of future New York City Mayor Dinkins. When a state senator died in 1985, Paterson was tapped to replace him. He was elected overwhelmingly in a special election, officially launching his political career.

During a decade of service in the state senate, Paterson earned the respect and admiration of his peers and constituents. His excellent performance and political skills helped him to move up the ranks in state government, and he became New York's youngest minority leader. Paterson was then chosen to run as lieutenant governor on the ticket of Democratic gubernatorial nominee Eliot Spitzer. The pair won that race in a landslide victory, and Paterson took office as lieutenant governor.

Not long after taking office, Governor Spitzer was forced to resign because of impropriety. Paterson took Spitzer's place as governor, becoming only the fourth African-American governor in U.S. history. Paterson served as governor from 2008 to 2010. He did not seek reelection to a full term.

PATRICK, DEVAL

GOVERNOR OF MASSACHUSETTS

1956

"Hope for the best and work for it."

As he was growing up in a crowded apartment on the south side of Chicago, Deval Patrick believed in a future for himself that was far removed from his humble beginning. Raised by his mother and grandparents, he performed well in school and demonstrated a natural ability to get along with other people. He was eager for a chance that would provide him with options for doing great things with his life.

He soon received that opportunity when one of his teachers helped him secure a scholarship to attend Milton Academy in Milton, Massachusetts, one of the leading private high schools in the country. Although moving away from home was difficult, Patrick quickly adjusted to the demands of his new environment and went on to attend Harvard University, where he earned a degree in English and American literature. He then spent a year in Africa working for the United Nations, before returning to Harvard for law school where he earned a law degree. Following a legal clerkship and work with the NAACP Legal Defense Fund, Patrick joined a law firm, got married, and began to focus on his family.

His first real taste of public life came when President Clinton tapped him to head the Justice Department's civil rights division. There he served as an assistant attorney general overseeing many high-profile cases for three-plus years. He made the switch back to corporate life, with high-level positions at Coca-Cola, Texaco, and the giant mortgage lender ACC Capital Holdings before turning his attention back to politics. Pursuing his lifelong passion for public service, he launched a "dark horse" campaign to become the governor of Massachusetts. Against tough competition, he succeeded in reaching his goal by earning a majority of the votes cast. He is the first and only African American to have served as governor of Massachusetts, holding office from 2007 to 2015.

During his two terms as governor, Patrick approved legislation for gun control and same sex marriage. He also supported programs to promote Massachusetts' life sciences industry, oversaw the expansion of affordable healthcare insurance to make it available to a majority of the commonwealth's citizens, and he made major reforms to Massachusetts' pension and transportation systems. Since completing his second and final term as governor, Patrick has returned to the private sector where he continues to do work that makes a positive change in the lives of others.

PINCHBACK, PINCKNEY BENTON STEWART ("P.B.S.")

GOVERNOR OF LOUISIANA

1837–1921

"We are an element of strength and wealth too powerful to be ignored by the American People. All we need is a just appreciation of our own power and our own manhood."

Pinckney Benton Stewart Pinchback (aka P.B.S. Pinchback) was the first person of African descent to become governor of a state in the United States. Pinchback served as the governor of Louisiana for 15 days, from December 29, 1872, to January 13, 1873, and he was later elected to the Louisiana State Legislature. He was also elected to the U.S. Senate, but he had his seat refused due to a political controversy fueled by racial tensions. He was the only African American to serve as governor of any state until 1990, when Douglas Wilder was elected governor of Virginia.

Born free in 1837, the son of a free slave and her former white enslaver, Pinchback was raised on his father's Louisiana farm as nearly an equal to his white brothers and sisters. As such, he received a quality education, and he was not subject to the abuse that was typical for Blacks during the time. After his father died, his mother moved the family to Ohio to avoid the possibility of being forced back into slavery. Because of these circumstances, Pinchback began working when he was only 12 years old as a cabin boy on Mississippi River steamboats.

When the Civil War broke out in 1861, Pinchback returned to New Orleans where he recruited men to serve in the First Louisiana Native Guard, one of the first all-Black regiments to fight in the Union Army during the Civil War. Commissioned a captain, he was one of the Union Army's few commissioned officers of African-American ancestry. He later resigned from that post after being denied promotions and experiencing ongoing prejudice from white officers.

After the war Pinchback took his father's surname of Pinchback, and he became active in the Republican Party. He then sought to take advantage of the new rights granted to Blacks under Reconstruction. He organized the Fourth Ward Republican Club in New Orleans and became part of the delegation that established a new constitution for the state of Louisiana in 1868. Later that year he was also elected to the Louisiana State Senate. Pinchback was very popular among his peers in the state capital, and he eventually became the state senate's president. When the lieutenant governor died unexpectedly, Pinchback was next in line to replace him. Then, when impeachment proceedings were initiated against Governor Henry Clay Warmouth, Pinchback was again next in line for that job. He replaced Warmouth and served as governor for less than a month.

After his brief time as governor, Pinchback was elected to Congress as a representative from Louisiana. Unfortunately his seat was contested by a political rival, and because of growing white hostilities to Black achievements during Reconstruction, he was denied an opportunity to serve. Pinchback decided to leave politics, and he enrolled in law school. After passing the bar, he moved his family to New York City where he became a federal marshal. He later moved to Washington, D.C., where he remained active in politics until his death in 1921.

WILDER, LAWRENCE DOUGLAS
GOVERNOR OF VIRGINIA

1931

"You don't ever earn a right to stop doing anything if you feel there is an obligation to move in terms of public service."

Lawrence Douglas Wilder was the first African American to be elected governor of the Commonwealth of Virginia. He was also the first African-American governor of any state since Reconstruction. While governor, he was credited for sound economic management that balanced the state budget during difficult economic times. During his time as governor, Wilder was also the highest-ranked African American elected official in the United States.

Named after abolitionist Frederick Douglass and poet Paul Lawrence Dunbar, Wilder was born in Richmond, Virginia. As a child of the Great Depression, his parents stressed education as a way to improve quality of life. While attending Virginia Union University, he waited tables at hotels. After earning his degree in 1951, he was drafted into the U.S. Army where he earned the Bronze Star during the Korean War.

Following the war, Wilder entered Howard University Law School and earned a law degree. He then set up a law practice in Richmond. Leveraging his reputation for strong leadership ability, he entered politics, winning a seat in the Virginia State Senate in 1969. After sixteen years in the state Senate, he was elected lieutenant governor, before going on to the top job in 1989 when he was elected governor.

"The force I represent is Virginia's New Mainstream," Wilder said at his inaugural, taking his oath outside the state's Capitol, a building that had served as the Confederate Capitol during the Civil War. "It looks forward, not backwards. It tries to unify people, not divide them."

While in office, Wilder prioritized crime and gun control. He also worked to improve the transportation system throughout Virginia. He proposed legislation that stopped investments in apartheid, making Virginia the first Southern state to take such action. After serving four years, Wilder left office due to Virginia's term limit policy.

Since leaving the governor's office, Wilder has pursued many of his passions, such as hosting a radio show and teaching public policy at Virginia Commonwealth University. After a decade away from politics, he returned to serve as mayor of Richmond from 2005 until 2009.

Wilder continues to remain active in politics and oversees the L. Douglas Wilder School of Government and Public Affairs at Virginia Commonwealth University.

U.S. SENATORS

"This country has profound and pressing social problems on its agenda. It needs the best energies of all its citizens, especially its gifted young people."

—Senator Edward W. Brooke from a commencement speech given at Wellesley College, 1969

BOOKER, CORY

U.S. SENATOR FROM NEW JERSEY

1969

"All of us need to be committed to living our authentic truth and be willing to give things up, sacrifice in life to better achieve who we are called to be."

Cory Booker has always been a high achiever and well liked. He was born in Washington, D.C., but grew up in a tight-knit middle-class family in Harrington Park, New Jersey. He was also very compassionate, and he believed that it was important to use his talents to help others.

"My parents taught me to whom much is given, much is expected," he once said. "So even at the earliest ages, I found myself playing the role of the big brother, the guy who was trying to look after people."

After high school, Booker attended Stanford University in California where he played varsity football and was active in student government. He continued his education as a prestigious Rhodes Scholar at the University of Oxford in England, one of the oldest colleges in the world. While earning a law degree from Yale University in 1997, he ran a free legal clinic for low-income residents.

"All my life I've fantasized about fighting the good fight. It's all about energy, and the more you throw positive energy and unconditional love in the world, the more it's gonna hit and stick."

Booker knew that he wanted to pursue a career doing advocacy work. After completing law school, he moved to Newark, New Jersey, where he started a nonprofit. It was at this point that he began to consider entering politics.

"I knew that I could get more accomplished if I were a part of the political structure," he said. "I decided to run for a seat on the city council to better understand how things work, so that I could change them."

During his time on the city council (1998–2002), Booker sponsored initiatives that addressed housing issues, young people, and law and order, which gained him enormous respect from the citizens in his district. After his term ended, he decided he could further his mission to help the citizens of Newark as the city's mayor. Although he lost during his first try, he reinvested his energy and ran again in 2006, this time winning a majority of the vote. He was elected to a second term as mayor in 2010.

In 2013, Booker defeated Republican challenger Steve Lonegan to become the first African American elected to the Senate from New Jersey.

"I am here because I believe people who care can find solutions to even the most difficult problems," he said. "I am here because, when we work together, I know from experience that there are no problems we can't solve. I know that I am capable of doing great things for my state and for this nation."

BRAUN, CAROL MOSELEY

U.S. SENATOR FROM ILLINOIS

1947

"I want to rebuild America."

Carol Moseley Braun has achieved many firsts during her long and distinguished career. She was the first Black woman elected to the U.S. Senate. She was also the first African American elected to the senate from Illinois.

Born in Chicago, Illinois, Moseley Braun is the oldest of four, and grew up in a middle-class family. She developed a passion for politics early on and earned a bachelor of arts degree in political science from the University of Illinois in 1969. While attending the University of Chicago School of Law, she worked on the campaigns of future Chicago mayor Harold Washington (then an Illinois state representative) and Illinois State Senator Richard Newhouse, before embarking on a career of her own.

After working as a prosecutor in the U.S. Attorney's office in Chicago, Moseley Braun took the plunge into politics, winning a seat in the Illinois House of Representatives in 1978. During her decade in the state legislature, she rose through the ranks to become the assistant majority leader. She was elected Cook County Illinois, recorder of deeds in 1988, becoming the first African American to hold an executive position in Cook County, before mounting a successful campaign for the U.S. Senate. She assumed her seat in 1999.

As a senator, Moseley Braun became known as an advocate for social change, working for reforms in education, government, and healthcare. She was also a very vocal supporter of women's rights and civil rights. During her time in office she was active on the powerful Senate Finance Committee, the Senate Judiciary Committee, and the Senate Banking, Housing, and Urban Affairs committees. Moseley Braun supported educational reforms and called for more restrictive gun control laws. Highlights of her time in office included sponsoring the creation of the Sacagawea coin to recognize women of color and the National Park Service initiative to fund the historic preservation of the Underground Railroad.

After serving one full term in office, Moseley Braun lost her bid for reelection. In 1999, she was appointed ambassador to New Zealand by President Bill Clinton. Following that post, she made unsuccessful attempts to run for U.S. president and then mayor of Chicago, before retiring completely from politics. Today she runs a private law firm and is the CEO of an organic food line.

BROOKE, EDWARD W.

U.S. SENATOR FROM MASSACHUSETTS

1919–2013

"My entire life has been devoted to breaking down barriers, to finding common ground."

When Edward Brooke was elected to the U.S. Senate from Massachusetts, he ended an 85-year absence of African-American senators in Congress. He was the first African American elected to the U.S. Senate by popular vote. The first African Americans to serve in the Senate, Hiram Revels and Blanche K. Bruce, both from Mississippi, were elected by their state legislatures, which was the process during the 1800s in their state.

Born in Washington, D.C., Brooke graduated from Howard University in 1941 and then enlisted in the U.S. Army after the attack on Pearl Harbor. Following his discharge, he enrolled at Boston University School of Law. After graduating, he started his own law firm in the Roxbury section of Boston. At the urging of friends, he began to pursue a career in politics, setting his sights on a seat in the Massachusetts House of Representatives. He won in the Republican primary, but he lost in the general election. A second attempt was also unsuccessful as well as a run for secretary of state.

But Brooke didn't give up. A run for attorney general of Massachusetts was successful, and in 1962 he became the first African American elected to that post in any state in the country. In 1965, he announced his candidacy for the U.S. Senate. He was opposed by former governor Endicott Peabody, but Brooke won the race handily, becoming the first African American elected to the Senate since the Reconstruction era.

As a senator, Brooke was a leading advocate against discrimination in housing, and he worked on behalf of affordable housing. He coauthored the 1968 Fair Housing Act, which prohibited discrimination in housing and created the Department of Housing and Urban Development (HUD) Office of Fair Housing and Equal Opportunity. Brooke also blocked attempts to close down the Job Corps and the Office of Economic Opportunity, and attempts to weaken the Equal Employment Opportunity Commission (EEOC).

Although Brooke was a member of the Republican Party, he often adopted a liberal agenda with regard to social issues. He fought hard for the expansion of the Voting Rights Act, and he supported legalized abortion rights for women. The latter issue cost him badly in his heavily Catholic commonwealth, and it contributed to his failure to be reelected after serving two terms.

After leaving office, Brooke returned to his law practice, and continued to advocate for causes important to him. Diagnosed with breast cancer in 2002, he returned to the public spotlight to increase awareness of the disease in men. For his work as a public servant, he was awarded the Presidential Medal of Freedom (2004) and the Congressional Gold Medal (2009).

BRUCE, BLANCHE K.

U.S. Senator from Mississippi

1841–1898

"I have confidence, not only in this country and her institutions, but in the endurance, capacity, and destiny of my people."

Blanche Bruce was a former slave who became a successful farmer and then a U.S. Senator. The second African American to serve in the Senate and the first to be elected to a full term, he dedicated his political life to advocating and protecting the rights of African Americans and others.

Bruce was born in Virginia, the son of an enslaved African-American woman and the owner of a plantation. Because he was the son of the man who owned him, Bruce enjoyed a greater degree of freedom than most Blacks of his time. But he was still enslaved. He was educated with his White half-brother, and when he was old enough, his father arranged for an apprenticeship so Bruce could learn a trade. A few years after the Civil War started, he ran away to Kansas where he attempted to enlist in the Union Army. His application was denied. So he traveled about, taking on various jobs including teaching, establishing a school for Black children, and working as a steamboat porter. In 1868, he relocated to Mississippi and became a successful farmer, acquiring more than 640 acres of land.

Bruce soon caught the eye of the Republican leadership, which was made up of both Black and White citizens, and they tapped him for his first political position as registrar of voters. Eventually he became one of the most-recognized politicians in the state. His success as a Black politician was unprecedented: he was elected to the joint office of sheriff and tax collector, and he was appointed county superintendent of education. In 1874, the state legislature elected him to a full six-year term as a U.S. senator.

During his term in Congress (1875–1881), Bruce fought for equal rights and justice for African Americans. He sought to integrate the U.S. Army. The fiery senator presided over the Republican National Conventions in 1880 and 1888, receiving vice presidential nominations both years.

The climate in the country changed after Reconstruction when federal troops who had been protecting the rights of African Americans were removed from the South. Jim Crow laws that robbed African Americans of their rights as citizens were enacted, and those laws included some that prohibited Blacks from voting and holding office. Bruce would be the last African-American member of Congress for many decades.

After leaving the Senate, Blanche K. Bruce was selected as recorder of deeds in Washington, D.C., and registrar of the U.S. Treasury, a position he held when he died in 1898.

HARRIS, KAMALA

U.S. Senator from California

1964

"I was raised to be an independent woman, not the victim of anything."

Kamala Harris was destined to be a winner. The daughter of an Indian (East Asian) mother and a Jamaican father, Kamala was born in Oakland, CA, during the turbulent 1960s. She learned very early the importance of fighting for justice, which would lead to her role as chief attorney in California, the most populous state in the country.

Harris was good student who was very aware of her responsibility to others.

"My parents were very much a part of the Civil Rights Movement, so growing up I was surrounded by people who were passionately fighting for changes to our society," she said. "Ultimately, I was inspired to make my own contribution to this noble cause by achieving academically and then through public service."

After graduating from high school, Harris attended Howard University (1982–1986) where she was active in student government and social issues. Upon her return to the Bay Area, she earned a law degree from the University of California, Hastings College of Law (1986). There, she set her sights on a career in public service.

"From the very beginning I had a strong sense of my values, and therefore I knew that I was destined to use my talents to make a difference in other people's lives."

She began her career in the Alameda County District Attorney's Office, where she worked as a deputy district attorney from 1990 to 1998. In the following years, she served as the managing attorney in the Career Criminal Unit of the San Francisco District Attorney's Office, then as chief of the Community and Neighborhood Division in the Office of the San Francisco City Attorney.

In 2003, she ran for district attorney of San Francisco. Harris won that election and was reelected in 2007. Three years later, she set her sights on the attorney general post. She won that election too, and she was reelected in 2014 to a second term. Harris is the first African American and first Asian American to serve as attorney general of California.

In November 2016, Harris made history. California voters chose her to become the first Indian-American and second African-American female elected to serve in the U.S. Senate.

"Whatever the results of the presidential election tonight, we know that we have a task in front of us. We know the stakes are high," Harris told a cheering crowd inside Exchange LA during her victory speech. "When we have been attacked and when our ideals and fundamental ideals are being attacked, do we retreat or do we fight? I say we fight!"

REVELS, HIRAM RHODES

U.S. SENATOR FROM MISSISSIPPI

1827–1901

"Let no encouragement be given to a prejudice against those who have done nothing to justify it."

Hiram Rhodes Revels was the first African American chosen to serve in Congress. Elected senator only five years following the end of slavery, Revels's achievement represented an important breakthrough for African Americans. The new political freedom, however, would not last long.

Born in Fayetteville, North Carolina, to free parents of color, Revels was tutored by a Black woman. In 1838, when he was 11 years old, he was sent to live with his older brother who taught him the barber trade. After attending Union County Seminary in Indiana and Drake County Seminary in Ohio, he was ordained as a minister in the African Methodist Episcopal (AME) Church.

From 1845, when he was ordained, until 1855, Revels, with his wife and family, traveled to Indiana, Illinois, Kansas, Kentucky, and Tennessee preaching the Gospel and teaching fellow African Americans. From 1855 to 1857, Revels attended Knox College, becoming one of a few Black men in the United States at the time with some college education.

When the Civil War broke out in 1861, Revels helped recruit two Black regiments from Maryland. He also served as the chaplain for a Black regiment that fought in Vicksburg and Jackson, Mississippi. During Reconstruction, Revels was elected alderman in Natchez, and was elected to represent his home county in the Mississippi State Senate where he was one of 30 African Americans. During this time, legislatures in most states elected their U.S. senators.

An accomplished orator, in 1870, Revels presented the opening prayer in the Mississippi State Legislature. One legislator called the prayer one of the most "impressive and eloquent prayers that had ever been delivered in the Mississippi Senate chambers." Later that year, Revels's fellow legislators elected him to complete the term of another U.S. senator. Some Democratic senators in Washington did not want to seat their new colleague. Attempting to resuscitate the Dred Scott Supreme Court decision, they claimed that African Americans were not citizens and therefore could not hold political office. After two days of debate, Revels received enough votes to take his seat. He served in the Senate from February 1870 to March 1871. Discouraged by the prejudice and difficulty he faced in the U.S. Senate, he resigned two months before his term expired and accepted an appointment as the first president of Alcorn A&M, a historically Black institution located in Mississippi.

SCOTT, TIMOTHY EUGENE

U.S. SENATOR FROM
SOUTH CAROLINA

1965

"The circumstances that surround you are less important than the potential in you."

Growing up poor in the inner city of Charleston, South Carolina, Timothy Scott always had a sense of hope in his future. Even though he struggled academically, he was encouraged by his mom, grandmother, and teachers to reach the leadership potential they saw in him. Scott achieved despite tremendous odds, becoming the first African American from the Deep South to serve in the U.S. Senate since Reconstruction, representing his home state of South Carolina.

"I was raised to believe that if I sought to be average, then I was going to get a little less," he has said. "So I decided to aim for the moon because I knew that even if I missed that, I would still be among the stars in the sky."

Although he was deeply committed to creating a better life, Scott's dreams for success were almost derailed after he nearly flunked out of high school. Fortunately, due to the positive influence from his family and the other adults in his life, he got through, earning a partial scholarship to attend college.

"I ran into some difficult periods in my early life, but I was lucky that I had great role models who provided me with the kind of example to follow. What I learned is that even when life is not easy, I have to keep trying to do my best."

After receiving a bachelor's degree from Charleston Southern College in 1988, Scott embarked on a career in business, selling insurance and real estate. He also began to volunteer for various causes and political campaigns in his local community. It was also around this time that he became a member of the Republican Party. Although African Americans in recent years have not played a major role in the party, Scott's reasons for joining the party were deeply personal.

"I became a member of the Republican Party because I believe in the core values that the party represents," he said. "I also believe that America is at its best when we work together, and as a politician I want to work with everyone to achieve what's best for this nation."

Scott served on the Charleston County Council for 13 years and became the council's chairperson. He then became the first African American elected in more than 100 years to the South Carolina House of Representatives. After one term in office, he was elected to the U.S. House of Representatives. Scott made history in 2012 when South Carolina's governor Nikki Haley appointed him to fill the Senate seat being vacated by retiring Senator Jim DeMint. Scott's appointment made him one of only eight African-American senators in U.S. history. Scott was elected to the U.S. Senate in November 2016.

U.S. REPRESENTATIVES

"The scars and stains of racism still remain deeply embedded in American society, whether it is stop and frisk in New York or injustice in [the] Trayvon Martin case in Florida, the mass incarceration of millions of Americans, immigrants hiding in fear in the shadow of our society, unemployment, homelessness, poverty, hunger, or the renewed struggle for voting rights."

—U.S. Representative John Lewis, Georgia
from a speech delivered August 28, 2013 at the
Lincoln Memorial during a ceremony to commemorate
the 50th anniversary of the March on Washington

BURKE, YVONNE BRATHWAITE
U.S. REPRESENTATIVE FROM CALIFORNIA

1932

"I came along at a time when there was a demand to give men greater visibility and opportunity. In White society they were saying, 'Women can't do it.' In Black society they were saying, 'Women do too much.' It's a diabolical situation."

Yvonne Brathwaite Burke was already a rising star in California and national politics when she won a seat in the U.S. House of Representatives. She was the first African-American woman elected to the California State Assembly, and soon after that she gained national television exposure with her leadership position at the 1972 Democratic National Convention. That same year she became the first Black woman from California (and one of only three Black women ever) elected to the U.S. House.

Born in Los Angeles, California, in 1932, she grew up an only child in a family of modest means. A natural leader, she was elected vice president of her senior class in high school. She earned a political science degree from UCLA, and went on to attend the University of Southern California (USC) Gould School of Law where she was one of the first Black women ever admitted. While there she demonstrated tremendous leadership skills when she organized a rival student club after she had been denied membership in another club because of her race. After graduating and passing the bar, she once again exhibited a spirit of endurance. She started her own law practice when she discovered that no firms in the entire state would hire her due to her gender and race.

Using the experience she gained working as deputy commissioner with the state of California and as a hearing officer for the Los Angeles Police Commission, in 1966, Burke won election to the California State Assembly. Her political career blossomed from there, and after three terms, she successfully campaigned for a seat in the U.S. House of Representatives. In the House, Burke earned a reputation as a legislator who avoided confrontation and worked effectively behind the scenes to effect changes she believed were most important. During her time in Congress, she received assignments on numerous committees. She was also selected for a seat on the powerful Appropriations Committee. Burke thrived in her position as a leader and role model, and she encouraged young people to pursue their dreams. She often told constituents, "No matter what is in your way, never give up. Chase after your dream, with no interference of discouragement."

Burke served in Congress from 1973 to 1979. She decided not to run for another term but instead returned to California where she was appointed by the governor to the University of California Board of Regents and later to the L.A. County Board of Supervisors. She eventually became the first woman and the first person of color to chair that board. Burke announced her retirement after 16 years on the board. Today she has largely left political life and resides with her family in Los Angeles.

CHISHOLM, SHIRLEY

U.S. REPRESENTATIVE FROM NEW YORK

1924–2005

"You don't make progress by standing on the sidelines, whimpering and complaining. You make progress by implementing ideas."

During her career, Shirley Chisholm made history twice: first, as the first African-American woman elected to the U.S. Congress and second, as the first major-party Black candidate to make a bid for the U.S. presidency. Known for her strong leadership abilities and her deep commitment to social causes, she earned the respect of her peers in both parties and established a performance benchmark that future generations of politicians strive to reach.

Born to Caribbean immigrant parents in Brooklyn, New York, Chisholm was the oldest of four siblings. In 1929, when she was five, she and two of her sisters were sent to live with their grandmother on a farm in Barbados. When she returned to Brooklyn five years later, Chisholm spoke with a recognizable accent that she retained for the remainder of her life. Always a good student, Chisholm earned a bachelor's degree from Brooklyn College in 1946, then a master's degree in elementary education from Columbia University. For a number of years, she worked in education. Then, in 1965, she ran for a seat in the New York General Assembly and won. In 1968, she ran for U.S. representative for her district. She won again.

In the House, Chisholm was assigned to the House Agricultural Committee, where she helped establish the Special Supplemental Nutrition Program for Women, Infants and Children (WIC). She also served on the Veterans' Affairs Committee, and later she won a much-prized position on the Education and Labor Committee. During her second term in the House, she decided to run for president because she wanted to create a platform that addressed the issues that affected the majority of American people. Her campaign received national attention, and she won a lot of support from students, women, and minority groups. Chisholm entered 11 primaries and campaigned in several states, securing important delegates to support her at the Democratic National Convention. Although she didn't win the nomination, her candidacy put a spotlight on the critical social and political issues that were important to her.

Following her presidential campaign, Chisholm returned to Congress. After 14 years in office, she retired, and she subsequently became a professor at Mount Holyoke, an all-women's college in Massachusetts. She also cofounded the National Political Congress of Black Women, an organization dedicated to the educational, political, economic, and cultural development of Black women and their families. She retired to Florida and passed away in 2005.

CLAY, JR., WILLIAM LACY
U.S. REPRESENTATIVE FROM MISSOURI

1956

"Following in his father's footsteps."

As a child growing up in St. Louis, William Lacy Clay, Jr. wanted to be like his dad, William Lacy Clay, Sr., a local community activist and businessperson who in 1969 became the first African American from Missouri elected to the U.S. House of Representatives.

Clay, Jr. spent his formative years in St. Louis with his parents and younger sister. He attended St. Francis Xavier grade school and filled his free time playing softball with his uncles and cousins and earned spending money shining shoes at the city's Lambert Airport.

After his father was elected to Congress, the young Clay moved with his family to Washington, D.C., where he attended Montgomery County public schools. He graduated from Springbrook High School in 1974 and attended the University of Maryland, where he earned a degree in political science.

Of his family's move to the nation's capital, Clay can still vividly recall his dad's swearing-in ceremony when, as his dad raised his right hand to take the oath of office, young Clay did as well. That experience, as well as others, such as his participation in nonviolent demonstrations in support of the Civil Rights Movement, left a lasting impression.

Following a period of youthful exuberance, during which Clay, Jr. hung out and hustled pool, the elder Clay encouraged his son to get back on the right track by securing him a job as a doorkeeper and security person for members of the U.S. House of Representatives. It was there that the younger Clay not only learned the names of all the members but more importantly, learned how laws were made.

Clay, Jr. returned to St. Louis with a mission to "impact people's lives in a positive way." He was elected to the Missouri House of Representatives in 1983, and in 1991, to the state senate. Following his dad's retirement in 2000, Clay, Jr. won a close election to replace his father as a member of the U.S. House of Representatives from Missouri.

Since then, William Clay, Jr. has been reelected five times by the citizens of his district. He has also served on a number of important committees in the House.

Commenting on his choice to follow in his father's footsteps, Clay, Jr. said: "Be sure that you want to serve the public before you enter into public life. When I decided to fill the giant shoes left by my father, I knew that I could only do the best job that I can do and have the people judge me on that."

CLYBURN, JAMES ENOS

U.S. REPRESENTATIVE FROM SOUTH CAROLINA

1940

"We have a moral responsibility to protect the earth and ensure that our children and grandchildren have a healthy and sustainable environment in which to live."

Leadership has always been a big theme in James Clyburn's life. Born into a family of activists, which was led by his minister father, Enos, and mom, Almeta, the South Carolina native has continued to illuminate his family's values as the number three Democrat in the U.S. House of Representatives. A national leader and champion for rural and big-city communities, he has worked to respond to the needs of America's diverse population.

Clyburn's leadership skills were evident at an early age. He was elected president of his NAACP youth chapter when he was 12 years old. While a student leader at South Carolina State College (an historical Black university), he helped organize many civil rights marches and demonstrations. After earning his degree in history in 1961, Clyburn taught school in Charleston where he fought to get college scholarships for needy students. He also became a community organizer who helped with hospital and garbage workers' strikes.

In 1971, in the aftermath of the student protests at South Carolina State in Orangeburg, where three African-American students were killed by South Carolina State Highway Patrol officers, then–governor John C. West appointed Clyburn to his staff. It was the first staff appointment of a minority by a South Carolina governor. Clyburn served in the position until 1992, when he decided to launch a campaign for a congressional seat.

He ran for a U.S. House seat in the newly drawn South Carolina Sixth Congressional District, and won the election. Clyburn was chosen co-president of the freshman class of representatives. He rose quickly through the ranks, establishing a liberal record on most issues.

In 2003, he was elected vice chairperson of the House Democratic Caucus, the third-ranking post in the caucus. Since entering that position, he has continued his support for higher education by leading the charge for increased Pell grants, programs in science and mathematics, and for historically Black colleges and universities (HBCUs). He has also championed economic development by securing funding for Empowerment Zones and investing in green technology development.

One of the most powerful people in Washington, D.C., Clyburn continues to shine light on his family's values—values that helped lead to his success.

COLLINS, CARDISS

U.S. REPRESENTATIVE FROM ILLINOIS

1931–2013

"We will no longer wait for political power to be shared with us. [We] will take it."

It was a tragedy that led Cardiss Collins into political leadership. On December 8, 1972, her husband, U.S. Representative George Washington Collins, was killed in a plane crash at Chicago's Midway Airport. Despite the enormous grief she felt as a result of her loss, Collins went on to become the first Black woman to represent the state of Illinois in the U.S. Congress.

Born in St. Louis in 1931, Collins moved with her family to Detroit, where she attended high school. After graduating, she moved to Chicago and took a job in a factory. She began taking night classes at Northwestern University where she earned a business certificate and a diploma in professional accounting. She then secured a position with the Illinois Department of Labor as a secretary and later with the Illinois Department of Revenue as an auditor. By this time she was married, and had an active role in her husband's various political campaigns, including his successful bid for a congressional seat in 1970.

During his time in Congress, George Collins established a reputation for diligence and was active in addressing the issues that affected his constituents. He died shortly after being elected to another term. His untimely death left his wife with a young son. The leadership of the Illinois Democratic Party approached Collins about filling her husband's seat. She decided to carry on her husband's work, and with the support of those who had supported her husband, she defeated her opponents easily.

Anxious to continue the work her husband began and deeply committed to providing better living and working conditions for the poor and middle class, Collins gained confidence in her new position, and went on to serve on various committees in the House. She was the first African American and woman selected as a Democratic whip-at-large.

For 24 years, Collins kept her seat in Congress, and her popularity among her peers earned her the top spot as chairperson of the prestigious Congressional Black Caucus (CBC). A longtime advocate of increasing breast cancer awareness, she drafted legislation to help elderly and disabled women receive Medicare coverage for mammograms, and she introduced a law designating October as National Breast Cancer Awareness Month. Cardiss Collins died in 2013. The United States Postal Services Cardiss Collins Processing and Distribution Center in Chicago was named in her honor.

CONYERS, JR., JOHN

U.S. REPRESENTATIVE FROM MICHIGAN

1929

"If we quickly cast aside our constitutional form of government, then the enemy will not be the terrorists, it will be us."

For 50 years, John Conyers has represented his Michigan district in Congress. Elected to office at the very height of the Civil Rights Movement, Conyers has helped steer American politics through major social and political changes. Known as a strong defender of civil and human rights, Conyers has advocated on behalf of poor and underrepresented communities for almost all of his political life.

Conyers was born in Detroit, Michigan. His dad was an auto factory worker who helped organize one of the first African-American labor unions. Growing up, Conyers was heavily influenced by his dad's union activities, as well as the race riots that hit the city when he was a teen. Although music was his first passion, Conyers became motivated by the growing social activism in the country. Following high school, he worked in an auto plant in Detroit while attending college at night. He then enlisted in the Army and served in the Korean War. Upon returning home he enrolled at Wayne State University where he earned both a bachelor's degree (1957) and a law degree (1958).

After passing the bar exam, Conyers established his own law firm and began to develop a reputation in the community as an outstanding lawyer. From 1959 to 1961, he served as an assistant to U.S. Representative John Dingell, Jr. In 1964, he ran for a seat in the U.S. House of Representatives. He won that race, and he has held his seat in the House ever since, becoming the longest-serving African-American member of Congress in history.

Throughout his long political career, Conyers has been at the forefront of many of the issues that have dominated American life, including the Nixon Watergate investigation, and the creation of Dr. Martin Luther King, Jr., Day. He has also supported legislation for civil rights, women's rights, healthcare, and crime and gun control. A founding member of the Congressional Black Caucus, Conyers makes it a priority to mentor the next generation of Black elected officials. His many accomplishments and long history of service have earned him recognition by some of his peers as "Dean of the House."

"It is distressing to me that we live in an age in which we still must fight to protect our civil rights as Americans, in which a hate crime perpetrated against someone based on their sexual orientation can go unpunished, and in which discrimination is being written into our laws," Conyers once said.

CUMMINGS, ELIJAH EUGENE
U.S. REPRESENTATIVE FROM MARYLAND

1951

"We cannot allow it to be said by history that the difference between those who lived and . . . died . . . was nothing more than poverty, age, or skin color."

As one of the leading voices in the Democratic Party, Elijah Cummings has served as a member of the U.S. Congress for nearly 20 years. Representing parts of Baltimore, Maryland, and portions of northeast and central Maryland, Cummings is well respected on Capitol Hill, where he is known as a strong and progressive leader. He is equally recognized as a passionate advocate for a number of social and human rights issues.

A Baltimore native, Cummings graduated from Baltimore City College, a public magnet high school and one of oldest high schools in the United States. He gained his first taste of political life when he served as sophomore class president, student government treasurer, and student government president at Howard University. He earned his law degree from the University of Maryland School of Law in 1996.

After 19 years in private law practice, Cummings decided to pursue a career in politics, starting as a member of the Maryland House of Delegates where he served for 13 years, from 1983 to 1996. He was the first African American in Maryland history to be named speaker *pro tempore* of the Maryland General Assembly, which is composed of the House of Delegates and State Senate.

In 1996, Cummings beat a competitive field to win a seat in the U.S. House of Representatives, representing Maryland's Seventh District. During his terms in office he has served on numerous committees including the House Committee on Transportation and Infrastructure, the Subcommittee on Coast Guard and Maritime Transportation, and the Subcommittee on Railroads, Pipelines, and Hazardous Materials. Cummings is also a ranking member of the influential Committee on Oversight and Government Reform.

Dedicated to a life of public service, Cummings is very active in his community. He serves on the Morgan State University Board of Regents, the Baltimore Zoo Board of Trustees, and the Baltimore Area Council of the Boy Scouts of America Board of Directors. He also writes a biweekly column for the *Baltimore Afro-American* newspaper—one of the leading Black newspapers in the country.

"I believe that I can best serve the people of our nation by continuing my work in Congress," he has said, "by continuing to touch people in every part of our great nation and making sure that they are treated fairly."

DELLUMS, RON VERNIE

U.S. Representative from California

1935

"Failure is not a crime. The crime is not trying."

Throughout his long and noteworthy political career, Dellums has been an outspoken critic of injustice and a hardline supporter of equal rights for Blacks, the LGBT community, women, and people of color. He has earned a reputation as a politically astute student of social activism and how its effective use can create change.

Born in Oakland, at a young age Dellums was influenced by the social activism of his parents and extended family. His uncle was an organizer of the Brotherhood of Sleeping Car Porters, one of the first labor organizations established by African Americans. His mother and many of his aunts and uncles were also very involved in various political and social causes. These role models inspired in him a spirit of activism.

Dellums received a bachelor's degree from San Francisco State (1960) and a master's degree in social work from the University of California at Berkeley (1962).

Following college, he held a number of positions in social work, which led to his involvement in community affairs and local politics in the Bay Area. At the urging of friends and members of the community, he sought and won a seat on the Berkeley City Council. Three years later, in 1970, he mounted a successful campaign for the congressional seat representing Oakland.

After assuming his seat, Dellums quickly set out to make things happen. During his first year he introduced more than 200 pieces of legislation.

Despite being labeled a radical, he refused to tone it down as he brought to the floor bills to stop the war in Vietnam, to end apartheid in South Africa, and end racism in the military. Although most of the bills were unsuccessful, he gained the respect of many of his peers who admired his courage to stand up for what he believed. He was also a founding member of the Congressional Black Caucus.

After nearly 30 years in Congress, in 1997, he resigned his House seat. But in 2006, he was recruited to run for mayor of Oakland, California. He won and served one term. Dellums remains engaged, sharing his perspective and world view when he is called to speak.

Ron Dellums served 13 terms as a member of the U.S. House of Representatives, representing California's Ninth Congressional District.

DE PRIEST, OSCAR STANTON

U.S. REPRESENTATIVE FROM ILLINOIS

1871–1951

"I've been elected to Congress the same way as any other member. I'm going to have the rights of every other member of Congress, no more, no less, if it's in the congressional barber shop or at a White House tea."

Born in Mobile, Alabama, to parents who were both former slaves, Oscar Stanton De Priest and his family were among the first wave of African Americans to move to the North in pursuit of greater opportunities. After first settling in Dayton, Ohio, still a young man, De Priest moved to Salina, Kansas to study bookkeeping at Salina Normal School. In 1889, he moved to Chicago where he settled permanently, working initially as a builder and then as a contractor and real estate agent.

As he became more successful, De Priest became active in Chicago city politics. He began by playing a behind-the-scenes role but later became more active as a member of the Board of Commissioners for Cook County, Illinois. Then he was elected to the Chicago City Council, becoming Chicago's first African-American alderman (1915–1917). He ran for alderman again in 1919 as a member of the People's Movement Club, a mostly African-American political organization he founded. Although he did not win, the People's Movement Club became one of the most powerful political groups in Chicago.

When Martin B. Madden, the White Republican representative for the district where De Priest lived died, the mayor of Chicago, William Hale Thompson, chose De Priest to replace Madden on the ticket. The election drew national attention, and De Priest's effort to become the first African American elected to the U.S. Congress in more than 30 years was challenged by segregationists from around the country. But on November 6, 1928, De Priest was elected.

As the lone African-American member of Congress, De Priest was keenly aware of what his position meant to other Blacks throughout America. So he tried to establish a model that future Black members could follow. De Priest introduced several anti-discrimination bills, and he backed a measure to hold states and counties responsible for the prevention of lynching. While holding office for three terms (1929–1935), he famously proclaimed that he had done more for Black Americans than any member of Congress since the time of President George Washington.

In 1934, De Priest lost his seat in Congress to another African American, Democrat Arthur Mitchell. The election reflected a political trend among Black Americans who had grown dissatisfied with the Republican Party, the party of President Abraham Lincoln, and had begun supporting the Democratic Party, the party of then–President Franklin Roosevelt and his New Deal policies.

De Priest returned to Chicago and continued in city politics, serving as a city council member from 1943 until 1947. He died in 1951 at the age of 80. Today his former home is a National Historic Monument, and a school in Chicago is named in his honor.

ELLISON, KEITH MAURICE

U.S. REPRESENTATIVE FROM MINNESOTA

1963

"Everybody counts, and everybody matters."

Growing up in a working-class community in industrial Detroit, Michigan, Keith Ellison was taught to value hard work, character, frugality, and public service. "My parents didn't accept weak and substandard efforts; they also never tolerated self-pity or blaming others for my problems," he recalled.

Those are values that he has found useful on his journey to become the first African American elected to Congress from the state of Minnesota.

The third of five boys, Ellison grew up in a tight-knit family with grandfathers who each taught him valuable life lessons.

"Both of my grandfathers were very kind and caring men," he recalls. "I learned from one the value of patience and discipline that come from being an athlete, and from the other, through his social advocacy, I learned to appreciate public action and service to others."

Ellison graduated from the University of Detroit Jesuit High School and Academy, and attended Wayne State University in Detroit. It was during this time that he converted from Catholicism to Islam.

"I investigated it, it worked for me, and it made me have a sense of inspiration and wonder, and so I became a Muslim. It's been working for me ever since."

Armed with a degree in economics (1987), Ellison moved to Minneapolis where he attended the University of Minnesota Law School. After graduation in 1990, he joined a top law firm where he specialized in litigating civil rights, employment, and criminal cases. Ellison then became the executive director of the nonprofit Legal Rights Center in Minneapolis, which specialized in the defense of indigent clients, before entering private practice again.

Ellison entered politics when he was elected to the Minnesota House of Representatives. Following two terms in office, in 2007, he ran for the seat he now holds in the U.S. House of Representatives.

"When I first was elected, I had to overcome some prejudice against Muslims in the post-9/11 world," Ellison recalls. "I won the election anyway because my constituents are fair people. Entering this office, I felt awesome responsibility, and I also felt that I absolutely had to come through for my district."

Ellison has gained a reputation for being active in legislation to create economic opportunities for all Americans. He has been a vocal opponent of the Iraq War, and he has played a leadership role in the crusade for human rights in the Sudan and around the world.

"My purpose in Congress is to promote peace, diplomacy, and development in America and around the world. I feel that I have the hopes and dreams of good decent people to look out for, and I strive each day to realize that goal."

FUDGE, MARCIA LOUISE
U.S. REPRESENTATIVE FROM OHIO

1952

"The fact that our country—the greatest country in the world—remains mired in race relations issues in the year 2014 is an embarrassment. If we are to learn anything from the tragic death of Michael Brown, we must first acknowledge that we have a race issue that we are not addressing."

Widely regarded for her smart, highly focused, and no-nonsense leadership, Ohio member of Congress Marcia Fudge has built her political career on her ability to get things done. An effective coalition builder with a proven ability to problem solve and work across party lines, Fudge has established an impressive track record as an ally for civil rights and women's rights.

Born in Cleveland, Ohio, Fudge moved with her family to the Shaker Heights area of town as a young girl. A popular student, she excelled academically and athletically as a member of the field hockey and volleyball teams. Following high school, Fudge earned a bachelor of science degree in business from Ohio State University (1973) and a law degree from the Cleveland-Marshall College of Law (1983). She then went to work as a law clerk before joining the local prosecutor's office of the greater Cleveland area. From there she went on to become the county director of budget and finance and also occasionally served as a visiting judge.

As word of her abilities grew, Fudge was hired as chief of staff by her friend and mentor, U.S. Representative Stephanie Tubbs Jones during Jones's first term in Congress. When Fudge completed that assignment, she returned home and was encouraged to pursue elected office, which she did with a successful run for mayor of Warrensville Heights. As the city's first female and first African-American mayor, Fudge was responsible for lowering debt of the Cleveland suburb and overseeing a sharp rise in residential and business development. She also worked with other areas of the city leadership to dramatically improve schools and infrastructure.

With the sudden and unexpected death of Stephanie Tubbs Jones in August 2008, Fudge was selected as her replacement by a committee of local Democratic leaders. Although she was first hesitant to replace her friend, she accepted the seat to preserve and continue Jones's political legacy. She went on to serve out the balance of Jones's term in office, before mounting a reelection campaign that she won based on her own merit. Fudge has remained in Congress ever since, where she has earned the respect of her colleagues and constituents. During her time in Congress, she has served on the Committee on Agriculture and the Committee on Science, Space, and Technology. She is also a member of the Congressional Arts Caucus, the Congressional Progressive Caucus, and the Congressional Black Caucus.

JORDAN, BARBARA

U.S. REPRESENTATIVE FROM TEXAS

1936–1996

"There is no obstacle in the path of young people who are poor or members of minority groups that hard work and preparation cannot cure."

Barbara Jordan was a pioneer in American politics. She was the first African-American state senator in Texas, the first woman and first African American elected to Congress from Texas, and the first African-American woman to deliver a keynote address at the Democratic National Convention (1970).

The youngest of three sisters, she was born in Houston, Texas, on February 21, 1936, into a working-class family. Although her own family's life was nurturing, she had to face challenges because she was Black, female, and a large girl for her age. So she focused on education and became a standout student, particularly in speech and debate. After high school, she earned a bachelor's degree from Texas Southern University (1956) and a law degree from Boston University (1959).

Jordan's interest in politics began when she campaigned for presidential candidate John F. Kennedy and vice presidential candidate Lyndon B. Johnson, a fellow Texan, in the 1960 election. Soon, she began to pursue a political career of her own, first running unsuccessfully for a seat in the Texas House of Representatives in 1962, before winning a seat in the Texas legislature in 1966. While in office, she established a record as a determined and fierce fighter for the issues she valued. In 1972, she decided to run for a seat in the U.S. House of Representatives, and she won with an overwhelming 80 percent of the vote.

As Jordan made her transition to Washington, she was aided by former President Johnson. With his help she secured a position on the powerful House Judiciary Committee. Her talent as a speaker and lawyer was on display in 1974 when the committee was empowered to investigate whether there were sufficient grounds to impeach President Richard M. Nixon because of his involvement in the Watergate scandal.

Jordan served three terms in Congress. A strong advocate for civil rights, she helped sponsor legislation that broadened the provisions of the 1965 Voting Rights Act to include Hispanic Americans, Native Americans, and Asian Americans. Jordan also chaired the U.S. Commission on Immigration Reform, and vigorously supported legislation to require banks to lend and make services available to underserved poor and minority communities.

When she declined to seek a fourth term in office, Jordan was appointed the Lyndon Johnson Chair in National Policy at the LBJ School of Public Affairs at the University of Texas in Austin, and she lectured widely on national affairs. By the time of her death, in 1996, she had received many honors and recognition for her contributions, including the Presidential Medal of Freedom.

LEE, BARBARA JEAN

U.S. REPRESENTATIVE FROM CALIFORNIA

1946

"Let us not become the evil that we deplore."

With a well-earned reputation for standing up for the underserved and underrepresented, Congresswoman Barbara Jean Lee has represented California's Thirteenth Congressional District, which includes Oakland, California, for 15 years. As the only member from both chambers of Congress to vote against the use of military force in the wake of the terrorist attacks in the United States on September 11, 2001, Lee demonstrated her full commitment to a set of leadership principles and beliefs that earned her a nationwide spotlight.

A native of El Paso, Texas, Barbara Lee grew up in a military family that settled in southern California when she was in her teens. Following high school, she lived on public assistance as a single mother of two sons. Later, she entered Mills College where she earned a bachelor's degree in 1973. She went on to earn a master's degree in social work from the University of California at Berkeley (1975). While attending Mills College, Lee emerged as a leader in the student movement. She became a volunteer with the Oakland chapter of the Black Panther Party Community Learning Center. When Bobby Seale, one of the founders of the Black Panthers, decided to run for mayor of Oakland in 1973, Lee was a member of his staff.

Motivated by a passion to make a difference in her community, Lee continued to be involved in politics, joining the staff of U.S. Representative Ron Dellums. She started as an intern, and her hard work and dedication were rewarded when she became the congressman's chief of staff.

Lee's own political career began in 1990 when she was elected to the California State Assembly. Six years later, she was elected to the California State Senate.

When Congressman Dellums retired in 1998, Lee ran to succeed her former boss in the U.S. House of Representatives. She has held that office ever since. In 2008, she was elected chair of the Congressional Black Caucus.

During her years in Congress, Lee has been a champion for a wide range of causes such as education, social work, and healthcare. She has also been a very active congressional member who builds coalitions with other members across party lines to achieve positive outcomes on issues that are essential to America's welfare. A recipient of many accolades and honors recognizing her leadership, she is cochair of the Congressional Progressive Caucus and was nominated by President Obama to represent the U.S. Congress at the United Nations.

LEE, SHEILA JACKSON

U.S. REPRESENTATIVE FROM TEXAS

1950

"We must never rest and never stop. The generation that lives today must fight for equality of all Americans and help [ensure] all voices will always be heard."

U.S. Representative Sheila Jackson Lee is known for her boundless energy and deep commitment to the rich tradition of African-American activism. She is well known in national politics and currently represents the Eighteenth District in Texas, which includes much of Houston's inner city and the surrounding area.

A native of Queens, New York, Jackson Lee was an excellent student who also participated in many volunteer activities. After high school, she attended Yale University where she earned an undergraduate degree in political science in 1972. She received a law degree from the University of Virginia School of Law in 1975, and began work as an attorney, serving as staff counsel for the U.S. House Select Assassinations Committee from 1977 to 1978.

Jackson Lee and her husband then moved to Houston where, after three unsuccessful attempts, she secured a post as an associate municipal judge. In 1990, she was elected to a seat on the Houston City Council where she served for four years. In 1994, she was elected to represent her district in the U.S. House of Representatives, a seat once held by Barbara Jordan.

Since coming to Congress, Jackson Lee has strongly demonstrated her leadership abilities. She was elected president of her first-year class of Democrats in 1994, and she has held a leadership position with the Congressional Black Caucus. A well-known defender of the underdog, she has supported legislation for a number of important domestic issues in the areas of civil rights, juvenile justice, healthcare, and immigration. In international affairs, she has been a frontline advocate for improving America's trade position with China and finding a solution for the political unrest in Sudan. In an act of protest, Jackson Lee, along with four other members of Congress, were arrested while demonstrating in front of the Sudan embassy in Washington, D.C.

During her more than 20 years in office, Jackson Lee has been a ranking member of the Subcommittee on Crime, Terrorism, Homeland Security, and Investigations, and was the first woman to ever hold that position. She has also served on a number of committees and caucuses, including the House Committees on the Judiciary, Science, Homeland Security, and the 9/11 Commission Caucus, the Building a Better America Caucus, and the Congressional Human Rights Caucus.

LEWIS, JOHN ROBERT

U.S. REPRESENTATIVE FROM GEORGIA

1940

"You must be prepared if you believe in something. If you believe in something, you have to go for it."

Courage is an important leadership quality. U.S. Representative John Lewis has demonstrated that quality throughout his life. As a civil rights activist and leader and then as a member of Congress, Lewis has stood firm for causes time and time again. A son of the South, he has dedicated his life to fighting for justice and equality for African Americans, other people of color, the poor, and the dispossessed.

Lewis was born outside of Troy, Alabama, to a family of sharecroppers. Very early on, he faced the humiliation of segregation and racial discrimination that was so common in the daily lives of African Americans in the South and in many areas of the country. "White only" signs often made African Americans painfully aware that they were not allowed in hotels, eating facilities, bathrooms, schools, and other establishments and institutions. Most could not vote or hold public office either.

As a young boy, Lewis wanted to change the world he and other African Americans were forced to accept. Inspired by the Montgomery Bus Boycott and the words of Dr. Martin Luther King, Jr., he made a decision to be a part of the Civil Rights Movement.

While studying at Fisk University in Nashville, Tennessee, Lewis organized sit-in demonstrations at segregated lunch counters. In 1961, he participated in the Freedom Rides, which challenged segregated inter-state busing. From 1963 to 1966, he served as chairperson of the Student Nonviolent Coordinating Committee (SNCC), a leading civil rights organization. Only 23 years old in 1963, Lewis was one of the architects and keynote speakers at the historic March on Washington. Along with Dr. King, Whitney Young, James Farmer, Roy Wilkins, and A. Phillip Randolph, he was one of the "Big Six" leaders of the Civil Rights Movement.

Throughout the 1960s, Lewis continued to play an important role in the struggle for justice and equality in the South. He coordinated efforts to organize voter registration drives and community action programs. On March 7, 1966, he and Hosea Williams led more than 600 peaceful protestors across the Edmund Pettis Bridge in Selma, Alabama, to demonstrate for voting rights. Lewis was arrested 40 times, and he endured serious injuries on many occasions. But he was determined to stand up for the causes in which he believed. Many of the advances in civil and human rights over the last half century are due to his willingness to fight for a better America for all citizens.

In 1986, Lewis was elected to Congress, representing Georgia's Fifth District and has since earned a reputation as one of the most respected legislators in Congress. When John Lewis voices his concern about an issue, both Democrats and Republicans listen. He currently serves as senior chief deputy whip for the Democratic leadership in the House, and continues to fight for justice and equality.

LOVE, LUDMYA BOURDEAU ("MIA")

U.S. Representative from Utah

1975

"The America I know is great—not because government made it great but because ordinary citizens like me, like my father and like you, are given the opportunity every day to do extraordinary things."

Mia Love once had dreams of being an actress, but instead she has found her purpose in politics. She is the first Haitian American and the first Black female Republican in Congress, as well as the first African American to be elected to Congress from Utah. Widely considered a rising star in national politics, Love has also been credited with breaking stereotypes about Black women in public office.

A first-generation American, Love was born in Brooklyn, New York. Her family later moved to Norwalk, Connecticut, where her father worked various jobs in factories and drove a school bus and her mother worked as a nurse in a retirement home. Love was a dedicated student and fell in love with the performing arts while in high school. She attended the University of Hartford where she received a degree in fine arts in 1997.

While in college, Love was introduced to the Mormon faith.

"I had an older sister who had joined the religion, and while investigating the faith, I decided to join myself," she said. "I ended up wanting to be part of it because the Mormon faith just kind of worked for me."

Not long after graduating, she moved to Utah to stay with a friend. There, she joined a Mormon church, and in 1998, she married Jason Long whom she had first met in Connecticut where he served as a missionary.

As Love settled into family life, she became active in civic affairs, serving as a community spokesperson in Saratoga Springs, Utah, where her family resided. This led to a successful run for a seat on the city council, which she held for six years.

A firmly committed conservative, Love next ran a winning campaign for mayor of Saratoga Springs, a position she held for four years. During that time she began to gain national recognition, and she was an invited speaker at the 2012 Republican National Convention. Looking to take the next step in her political career, in 2012, Love mounted a campaign to win a seat in the U.S. House of Representatives. She lost narrowly to a more experienced politician. On her second try, November 4, 2014, she was successful, winning a seat to represent Utah's Fourth Congressional District.

NORTON, ELEANOR HOLMES

U.S. REPRESENTATIVE FROM WASHINGTON, D.C.

1937

"There is no reason to repeat bad history."

Eleanor Holmes Norton is a towering figure in American politics. A longtime civil rights and feminist leader, Norton is also a tenured professor of law, and has been a board member at numerous Fortune 500 companies. Also a fierce lawyer, she has defended both civil rights icon Julian Bond's and segregationist George Wallace's rights to free speech. Today, she is a delegate to the U.S. Congress representing the District of Columbia.

Norton was born and raised in Washington, D.C., by parents who were committed to her education and encouraged her to speak her mind about social injustice. She received a bachelor's degree from Antioch College in 1960, a master's degree from Yale University in 1963, and a law degree from Yale in 1964.

Throughout her undergraduate and graduate school years, Norton was active in the Civil Rights Movement. She was an organizer for the Student Nonviolent Coordinating Committee (SNCC), traveled to Mississippi to be a part of the 1964 Mississippi Freedom Summer Project, and worked with civil rights leader Medgar Evers. An early feminist, Norton contributed to the 1970 anthology *Sisterhood Is Powerful: An Anthology of Writings from the Women's Liberation Movement*, and was a founding advisory board member of the *Women's Rights Law Reporter*—the first periodical in the United States dedicated to women's rights law. Norton also endorsed the *Black Woman's Manifesto*, a classic document that represented the Black feminist movement.

After completing her academic studies, Norton worked as a law clerk for the Federal District Court. She then became assistant director of the American Civil Liberties Union (1965–1970), and chairwoman of the New York Human Rights Commission (1970–1977). President Jimmy Carter selected her to chair the U.S. Equal Opportunity Commission. She served in that capacity from 1977 to 1983.

In 1990, Norton was elected as a Democratic delegate to the U.S. House of Representatives for Washington, D.C. She is presently in her thirteenth term as a congressional delegate. As a representative from D.C., she is entitled to sit in the House of Representatives and vote in committee, but she is not allowed to vote on the final passage of any legislation on the legislative floor. The District of Columbia shares this limited form of congressional representation with Puerto Rico and four other U.S. territories: Guam, American Samoa, Northern Mariana Islands, and the U.S. Virgin Islands. In spite of this challenge, Norton has successfully supported initiatives that have increased home ownership and business opportunities in Washington, D.C. She has also served on the Committee on Oversight and Government Reform and the Committee on Transportation and Infrastructure. She is also an advocate for statehood for the District of Columbia.

PAYNE, JR., DONALD M.

U.S. Representative from New Jersey

1958

"We need people to be committed to the leadership in government, to continue to focus on those issues that we know are important."

Donald M. Payne, Jr. comes from a family of public servants. His father, Donald M. Payne, Sr. was the first African American elected to Congress from the state of New Jersey. His uncle William served in the New Jersey General Assembly as did another relative, Craig Stanley. So Payne Jr.'s life has always been filled with great expectations.

Much of Payne, Jr.'s early life was affected by the loss of his mom, who died from brain cancer when he was only five. Raised by his dad with the support of extended family, he was a good student and exceled in graphic arts. After completing high school, he attended Kean University.

Payne Jr.'s career in public service began when he founded Newark South Ward Junior Democrats and became its first president. His father, a leading voice for liberal causes, had set an early example of what it means to pursue public service as a career.

Payne, Jr. officially stepped into the political arena in 2006 when he was elected to the Newark, New Jersey Municipal Council in 2006. He served as its president from 2010 to 2012. He was also elected a freeholder-at-large for Essex County and served in that capacity from 2006 until 2012.

Tragedy struck the Payne family in March 2012 when Donald Payne, Sr. died. Although he was devastated by the loss of his father, Payne, Jr. declared his intention to run to fill the seat his father held for more than 20 years. He wanted not only to carry on his father's legacy but establish his own. After winning a special election to fill the remainder of his father's term, in November 2012, Payne, Jr. won in the general election.

Since being elected to represent New Jersey's Tenth Congressional District, Payne, Jr. has supported causes that are important to his constituents. He has demonstrated his leadership by supporting national and international initiatives as well.

Payne, Jr. believes that investing in our children is vital to their success and to the success of our economy. He introduced the *Promise Neighborhoods Act of 2013*, which encourages a holistic community-based approach to educating children in distressed neighborhoods, as well as the *SAFE in Our Schools Act of 2013* to better protect children and students in the event of emergencies. Congressman Payne, Jr. also fights for equal opportunities for foster care youth and students with disabilities, and he supports increased funding for Head Start and tuition-free community college for certain students.

After being elected to his first full term, Payne Jr. said, "I've said that I'm following a legacy, and I'm not backing away from that."

POWELL, JR., ADAM CLAYTON

U.S. REPRESENTATIVE FROM NEW YORK

1908–1972

"If you believe in a cause, you must be willing to put yourself on the line for that cause."

Once called the most militant man in Congress, Adam Clayton Powell, Jr. was a Baptist pastor who represented New York's Eighteenth District, which includes Harlem, from 1945 to 1971.

Powell, Jr. was born into a prominent family with a long history of social activism. His father, Adam Clayton Powell, Sr., was pastor of the prominent Abyssinian Baptist Church in Harlem—the third-oldest Black church in America. Following high school, Powell Jr. attended City College of New York before transferring to Colgate University, becoming one of only a handful of Black students at the institution. He planned to follow his father into the ministry and earned a master's degree in religious education at Columbia University in 1931.

Powell, Jr. joined his father at Abyssinian, preaching and assisting with charitable causes. He soon developed a dedicated following in New York City because of his crusades for jobs and affordable housing. In 1938, he succeeded his father as pastor of Abyssinian. Three years later he entered politics, becoming New York City's first African-American city council member. After one term in that office, he ran and was elected to the U.S. Congress on a platform that focused on civil rights.

Powell, Jr. was one of only two Blacks in Congress during this time (William Dawson from Illinois was the other). He championed a long list of social causes. A powerful and dynamic orator, he was known as "Mr. Civil Rights" among some of his peers in Congress. Some opponents, however, didn't appreciate the brashness and self-assurance coming from an African American.

After 15 years in Congress, in 1961, Powell Jr. became chairperson of the powerful House Education and Labor Committee. This committee proved enormously effective in helping to enact major parts of President John F. Kennedy's New Frontier and President Lyndon B. Johnson's New Society.

1n 1967, the U.S. House of Representatives stripped Powell, Jr. of his committee chairmanship because of alleged ethics violations. In 1968, it unseated him. But the voters in his district elected him to fill the vacant seat, and the U.S. Supreme Court ruled that the House had acted unconstitutionally when it refused to seat him. In 1970, the outspoken congressman lost a reelection bid to Charles Rangel, and shortly afterward he resigned as pastor of the Abyssinian Baptist Church. He retired from public life and moved to the island of Bimini, off the coast of Florida, where he died at the age of 63.

RANGEL, CHARLES B.

U.S. REPRESENTATIVE FROM NEW YORK

1930

"America was born as a nation of immigrants who have always contributed to its greatness."

New York Congressman Charles Rangel is a history-making politician, master lawmaker, and a founding member of the Congressional Black Caucus. He served 23 terms in the U.S. House of Representatives, and he is the first African-American member of Congress to lead the powerful Ways and Means Committee.

Rangel was born in Harlem. His father was Puerto Rican, and his mother was African American. He had a troubled family life, and after his dad left, Rangel learned how to take care of himself. Although he was a good student, he was not committed to schoolwork. He dropped out of high school at 16 and drifted aimlessly until he enlisted in the U.S. Army a year later.

Life in the military offered Rangel the structure he needed. During the Korean War, his skills as a leader emerged. Despite being injured, he led 40 of his comrades from behind enemy lines to safety. He was presented a Purple Heart and a Bronze Star.

After four years of military service he was honorably discharged from the Army, and returned home where he finished high school and used his GI Bill benefits to attend college. In 1960, he received a law degree from St. John's University School of Law. He held several legal positions before running successfully for a seat in the New York General Assembly in 1966. He served two terms. Then, in 1970, he challenged the iconic Adam Clayton Powell, Jr., and other candidates to represent the Eighteenth Congressional District in Congress and won.

When he arrived in Washington, D.C., Rangel focused on problems of importance to the Black community. He supported international causes such as trade and investment opportunities for struggling nations in the Caribbean and Africa.

Rangel served in the House of Representatives from January 1971 to January 2017. Among his proudest achievements is founding the Charles B. Rangel International Affairs Program in the U.S. State Department in cooperation with Howard University. More than 200 Rangel Fellows have completed the program, many serving as U.S. State Department Foreign Service officers in embassies around the world since the program began in 2002.

"The promise of the American Dream requires that we are all provided an equal opportunity to participate in and contribute to our nation," Rangel wrote in a 2013 blog in *Huffpost* titled, "The Struggle Continues for Civil Rights." The venerable political leader has dedicated his career trying to make that a reality for more Americans.

ROCHESTER, LISA BLUNT

U.S. REPRESENTATIVE FROM DELAWARE

1962

"One of the hallmarks of leadership, for me, is listening. It's pivotal. Even in this campaign, what we're doing is listening, going out to different parts of the state and listening."

In 1969, Ted Blunt brought his family, including his daughter Lisa, from Philadelphia to Wilmington, Delaware to work for Peoples Settlement Association, a social services organization more than a century old. He would carve out a career in public service that led to his becoming a member of the Wilmington City Council and eventually its president. So, it is not surprising that his dedication to public service would have an impact on his daughter. In the November 2016 election, Lisa Blunt Rochester made history, becoming the first woman and first African American elected to represent the state of Delaware in the U.S. Congress.

Blunt Rochester grew up in Wilmington and graduated from Padua Academy. Following high school, she attended Fairleigh Dickinson University in New Jersey, where she graduated with a bachelor's degree in international relations. Later, she received a master's degree in urban affairs and public policy from the University of Delaware.

Blunt Rochester began her professional career as a case worker for then–Delaware Congressman Tom Carper, helping people with Social Security benefits issues, disability insurance claims, IRS disputes, and housing needs. She served in the cabinets of two Delaware governors as Delaware's first African-American woman Secretary of Labor, and as Delaware's first African-American Deputy Secretary of Health and Social Services, and as State Personnel Director. She was also CEO of the Metropolitan Wilmington Urban League—an action-oriented, public policy research think tank focused on the inclusion of people of color.

This pioneering representative brings a lot of energy and zeal to her work, and is known for getting things done.

"We're kind of like a microcosm of the rest of the country, which gives people hope if you can do things here maybe we can do things across the country," Blunt Rochester said. "On the issue of jobs, on the issue of education, on the issue of women's health and the wage gap, people want real solutions and I have a history of doing that collaboratively with other people in the state."

SMALLS, ROBERT

U.S. REPRESENTATIVE FROM SOUTH CAROLINA

1839–1915

"My race needs no special defense, for the past history of them in this country proves them to be equal of any people anywhere. All they need is an equal chance in the battle of life."

Robert Small's life story sounds incredible, but it is remarkably true. At the height of the Civil War, Smalls led a crew of fellow slaves in a successful hijacking of a heavily armed Confederate transport ship, and they sailed it into the safety (and freedom) of a Union Army blockade. Following the war, he joined the ranks of first-generation Black politicians to be elected to the U.S. House of Representatives, where he served for five nonconsecutive terms.

Born into slavery in Beaufort, South Carolina in 1839, Smalls grew up influenced by his mother's Gullah culture. He spent his youth working in the home of his owner John McKee, who hired Smalls out to work in Charleston, South Carolina. Smalls worked a number of jobs, including as a dockworker, a rigger, a wheelman, and a sailmaker. Although McKee kept the money Smalls earned, Smalls became knowledgeable about the Charleston harbor and about sailing ships.

Following his marriage, Smalls was sent to serve aboard the *Planter*, a Confederate military transport ship that sailed along the South Carolina and Georgia coasts. He desperately wanted freedom for his wife and their two children and Smalls came up with a plan to use the ship to secure freedom for his family. On May 12, 1862, after recruiting seven of the other enslaved crewmen on board the ship, the men gathered their families and piloted the ship on a dangerous journey to freedom.

The courageous escape made Smalls famous, and he was hailed as a hero after turning the valuable ship over to the Union Army. With his family now free, he set about building a new life. He served as a pilot in the Union Navy, and later became the first Black captain of a vessel in the service of the United States. Because of Smalls's "great escape," he became a spokesperson for African Americans, which led to his career in politics.

Immediately following the Civil War, Smalls returned to Beaufort, where he purchased his former master's house and started a business. He became active in politics, serving in the South Carolina House of Representatives from 1865 to 1870 and then the South Carolina Senate between 1971 and 1874. In 1874, he was elected to the U.S. House of Representatives where he served from 1875 to 1879, 1882 to 1883, and 1884 to 1887. While in office, Smalls spoke boldly in defense of his race and also lobbied to end discrimination in many areas of American life.

Robert Smalls's contributions have been recognized and honored in many ways. His home in Beaufort has been designated a National Historic Landmark. In 2004, the U.S. Army named a ship, the USAV *Major General Robert Smalls* (LSV-8), in his honor. It is the only Army ship named after an African American. A five-mile section of South Carolina Highway 170, named the Robert Smalls Parkway, also stands as a tribute.

WATERS, MAXINE

U.S. REPRESENTATIVE FROM CALIFORNIA

1938

"I have a right to my anger, and I don't want anybody telling me I shouldn't be, that it's not nice to be, and that something's wrong with me because I get angry."

Throughout her years of public service, Maxine Waters has been a leading political voice, often tackling difficult and controversial issues. Representing California's Forty-Third Congressional District, which includes South Central Los Angeles, she has been a passionate advocate for women, children, people of color, and the poor. As one of the senior female members of the U.S. House of Representatives, the California congresswoman's strong legislative and public policy advocacy has been an example for a new generation of women in politics.

A native of St. Louis, Missouri, Waters and her 12 brothers and sisters were raised by their mother when their father left home. After finishing high school, Waters and her family moved to Los Angeles where she worked in garment factories and at a telephone company. While working as a teaching assistant for a Head Start program in South Los Angeles, Waters became interested in politics. She graduated from California State University, Los Angeles, and in 1973, she joined the staff of Los Angeles City Councilman David Cunningham as chief deputy.

Waters mounted her first election campaign in 1976 for a seat in the California State Assembly. She won by a large margin and served 14 years in the state assembly. When long-term congressman Augustus Hawkins, who had represented Waters's congressional district since 1963, announced his retirement in 1990, Waters was elected to replace him. She has served her district ever since, and she is the most senior of the African-American women in the U.S. House of Representatives.

Since her arrival in Washington, Waters has attracted national attention for her determined advocacy for the issues that impact her constituents and the country. She is former chair of the Congressional Black Caucus, a ranking member of the House Financial Services Committee, and a member of the Subcommittee on Oversight and Investigations. Waters's leadership continues to inspire her supporters and elicit the ire of some of her detractors.

"I've been in this struggle for many years now. I understand racism. I understand that there are a lot of people in this country who don't care about the problems of the inner city. We have to fight every day that we get up for every little thing that we get. And so I keep struggling," she said.

STATE LEADERS

"A leader inspires trust and confidence from friend and foe alike to take action that benefits all sides."

—The Honorable Willie L. Brown, Jr.
California Assembly Speaker 1980–1995

BRANDON, MARCUS

NORTH CAROLINA HOUSE OF REPRESENTATIVES

1975

"We need to move to a conversation that is more encompassing and representative of more people."

Marcus Brandon has been looking to create change all of his life. As a child living in a very conservative, White part of Guilford County, North Carolina, he was keenly aware of the different world in which he lived.

"I grew up in a very traditional family," he said. "My dad was a postal worker, and my mom did social work. They worked very hard to provide their family with advantages, and as a result we lived in an area that offered lots of opportunities. But I also had cousins who lived in the projects, which made me aware that there were big differences in the access that a person received based on where they lived, and I knew I wanted to change that."

Although Brandon wasn't the best student, he succeeded with the help of his parents' insistence on achievement. In addition to school, Brandon's education included volunteering for community activities such as door-to-door political campaigning. He attended North Carolina A&T State University where he majored in political science.

"I've been involved in political campaigns since I was 9 or 10 years old," he commented. "Doing that work definitely added to my real-life exposure because I would meet people who would share with me the challenges that they were facing in their lives. Those experiences fueled my passion and inspired me to be a voice for people who didn't have any."

As a young adult, Brandon was working for Hewlett-Packard when he decided to pursue a new direction. He moved to Washington, D.C., took a job with a large Democratic firm, and began working on campaigns across the country. He worked on behalf of many issues and candidates, gaining experience that would help him make his next move.

In 2010, Brandon ran for statewide office, seeking a seat in North Carolina's Sixtieth District. He defeated the Democratic incumbent and took office in 2011, serving until 2015.

As a gay Black man, Brandon is passionate about fighting any form of discrimination, and he is a vocal advocate for equal rights for all people. "My constituents are diverse, but many of their issues are the same," he has said.

After two terms in office, Brandon ran for the House seat vacated by former congressman Mel Watts. Although unsuccessful in his first attempt, his passion for politics still burns bright, and says he plans to run again.

BROWN, JR., WILLIE LEWIS
CALIFORNIA SPEAKER OF THE HOUSE

1934

"In politics, a lie unanswered becomes truth within 24 hours."

With a political history that includes eight years as the mayor of San Francisco (1996–2004) and another 31 years as a member of the California State Assembly, Willie Brown is widely regarded as one of the most successful politicians in American history.

Raised in East Texas during the depths of the Great Depression, Brown's early childhood was largely shaped by his mother and grandmother who instilled in him a strong work ethic at a young age. To help his family make ends meet, Brown worked as a shoeshine boy, a janitor, fry cook, and field hand. Following high school, he knew that his options were limited, so he moved to San Francisco, California, where he enrolled at San Francisco State University.

After graduating from San Francisco State University (1955) and the University of California Hastings College of Law (1958), Brown caught the spirit of political activism. He started one of the few Black law firms in San Francisco, where he often worked cases that involved civil rights violations. He then began organizing public protests, which gave him the confidence he needed to pursue a career in politics. While his first run for a seat in the California State Assembly failed, he ran again in 1964 and won.

Brown's personal style and keen political sense helped him rise through the ranks in California government. He successfully built coalitions that crossed Democratic Party lines, and cultivated a very loyal following among his constituents. He eyed the California Assembly's speakership position, and won the top seat in 1980. Brown's political connections and strong negotiation skills had given him nearly complete control over the California State Legislature by the time he became assembly speaker. Under his leadership, California passed legislation that required motorists to wear seat belts and increased educational and health testing standards (particularly for sexually transmitted diseases like AIDS). After 15 years in the assembly, Brown did not seek reelection to his seat and instead turned his attention to becoming the 41st mayor of San Francisco.

With his popularity and astute political skills, Brown easily won his race for mayor in 1996 and immediately put into motion plans to revitalize the city. During his two terms in office, he reduced crime, improved mass transportation, and help sponsor programs that radically decreased the city's homeless population. Since leaving office, Brown has remained a power broker in California. Today, he heads the Willie L. Brown, Jr., Institute on Politics and Public Service, where he shares his knowledge and skills with a new generation of California leaders.

HUGHES, VINCENT

PENNSYLVANIA STATE SENATE

1956

"Always do the right thing."

When Vincent Hughes was growing up in his West Philadelphia neighborhood, he felt that the possibilities for his life were limitless. Although the larger world around him was about to enter into the political and social turbulence that defined the 1960s, Hughes's formative years provided a sense of security that helped him develop the resilience and poise that have today made him one of Pennsylvania's most powerful senators.

"My mother was a staunch advocate for me and my sister, and my dad was constant and reliable," he said. "I always knew they had my back, and because of that I was fearless."

Young Hughes also benefited from his dedicated teachers and the community that he lived in, which was filled with thriving businesses and a rich tradition of progressive citizenship.

"I grew up in Philadelphia during a time when people were searching for opportunities that would move our community forward," he remembered. "I was well aware of the challenges that I would face as an African-American male, but the community had a solid backbone that gave me a sense of pride and empowerment."

After graduating from Temple University, Hughes worked as a library administrator at the University of Pennsylvania, and was an official of the District Council 47 of the American Federation of State, County, and Municipal Employees. He worked for a number of political campaigns where he cemented his resolve to pursue a career in politics. Although he failed at his first attempt in 1984 to win a seat in the Pennsylvania House of Representatives, he was not deterred. He won on his second attempt in 1986. He spent nearly a decade in the assembly, before **decid**ing it was time to seek a higher post.

"My mentor at the time was Chaka Fattah (then serving as a state senator), who decided that he was going to run for the U.S. House of Representatives. He saw my potential as a leader, and so he challenged me to run for his office."

In 1994, Hughes ran and won. Since becoming a state senator, he has built an impressive résumé. He has served as deputy minority whip, minority caucus secretary, and minority caucus chair, and he has been elected minority chair of the Appropriations Committee.

"I take pride in my reputation as a leader who handles issues that other people don't want to deal with," he said. "That position is something that I embraced, and it keeps me motivated to take on the huge responsibilities of my job and also inspire others to work for change and progress."

MUNICIPAL LEADERS

"I never had any question but that we would win. Now, as a professional politician, I'm always prepared to lose because I have both won and lost . . . races, but everything that I knew about the way in which that campaign was going and the information we were getting from our polling told me that we'd win, narrow though it might be, we would win."

—The Honorable Carl Stokes former mayor of Cleveland, Ohio
from an interview conducted by Blackside, Inc.,
October 28, 1988 for the documentary, "Eyes on the Prize"

BRADLEY, TOM
MAYOR OF LOS ANGELES, CALIFORNIA

1917–1998

"Never give up. Keep your thoughts and your mind always on the goal."

Tom Bradley was the longest-serving mayor in the history of Los Angeles. During his 20 years in office, he oversaw the city's radical transformation into a world-class city. As the city's first Black mayor, Bradley's election symbolized racial gains that were made in the aftermath of the Civil Rights Movement. Over his many years in office, his composed and focused manner made him a celebrated figure in the United States and around the world.

Bradley's family moved from Calvert, a small town in Texas, when he was seven years old and settled in Los Angeles, California. His father left, and a young Bradley had to work to earn money to help his family. An ambitious student, he excelled in track and field and earned an athletic scholarship to attend the University of California at Los Angeles (UCLA). At UCLA, he set records and became a team captain. Jackie Robinson was one of his classmates.

After graduating from college, Bradley joined the Los Angeles Police Department (LAPD) where he served as an officer for 21 years. When he reached the rank of lieutenant, the highest position an African American could achieve at that time, he attended Southwestern Law School at night, passed the bar, and became an attorney. With his law degree in hand, he resigned from the LAPD.

Bradley began to take an interest in politics. The local Democratic Party recognized his potential and encouraged him to run for public office. He did, winning a seat in 1963 on the Los Angeles City Council on his first try.

After two terms in office, Bradley set his sights on becoming mayor of Los Angeles. After an unsuccessful try in 1969, he formed a racially diverse coalition of supporters that helped him win in 1973, becoming the first African American elected to that office.

Bradley made a difference in Los Angeles. He opened city hall and city commissions to women, people of color, and people with disabilities. He helped transform Los Angeles from a conservative, White, urban center into one of the most diverse and important cities in the world. The city gained international attention when it hosted the 1984 Summer Olympics. But the uprising of 1992, sparked by the beating of Rodney King, an African American, by White L.A. police officers and their acquittal following a trial, also occurred during his administration.

After five terms in office, Bradley declined to seek a sixth. Tom Bradley died in 1996. A 1985 recipient of the NAACP's Spingarn Medal in 1985, the Tom Bradley International Terminal at the Los Angeles International Airport was named in his honor.

BROWN, AJA

MAYOR OF COMPTON, CALIFORNIA

1982

"I thought I could make change by just working at ground level, but to change a community you have to change policies. It's much easier to push from the top down than from the bottom up."

Growing up as a competitive and self-confident child, Aja Brown never doubted that she could fulfill her dreams.

"My mom worked hard to provide a security that motivated my brother and me to want to achieve. So from an early age I learned to live my life by the standards of excellence that she gave us."

Raised by a single mother in Altadena, California, Brown was a very active child who attended schools with students from different backgrounds. On weekends, she took college prep classes at Cal Tech and at a private girls' school. These experiences exposed her to a great diversity of opinions and ideas. She was also very active in a variety of extracurricular activities that stimulated her intellectually. But she had no interest in politics when she entered college. She earned a degree in public policy, urban planning, and development from the University of Southern California. A year later, in 2005, she earned a master's degree in urban planning with a concentration in economic development.

In 2006, Brown began working as an urban planner in the city of Inglewood. Three years later, she joined the Compton, California Redevelopment Agency as a redevelopment project manager, focusing her efforts on revitalizing the emergent city of Compton.

Armed with fresh ideas, limitless energy, and the firm belief that Compton needed a new direction, in 2013, Brown ran for mayor of the city. In a competitive race against 13 candidates, including the current mayor and a former mayor, Brown's message prevailed. At the age of 31, she became the youngest mayor in the city's history.

Since taking office, Brown's focus has been on improving education, creating accessible healthcare options, bringing new businesses to Compton, and working with churches and other organizations to effect lasting change. She plans to solicit the support of famous celebrities who were born or raised in Compton—Dr. Dre, Venus and Serena Williams, Kendrick Lamar, and others—to help accomplish her goal of transforming the city through fiscal reform, construction projects, jobs, health and wellness, and civic promotion. Brown believes that the citizens of Compton are no different from people in any other community, and she is determined to make sure the city can offer them the quality of life that they deserve.

DINKINS, DAVID
MAYOR OF NEW YORK, NEW YORK

1927

"I make the observation that no one of us would do things exactly alike."

As the first Black mayor of New York City, David Dinkins's focused leadership helped the nation's largest city recover from a harsh economic crisis and intense racial division. His election, a close race, reflected the high level of division and controversy that threatened to destroy the city. But as mayor of one of the most diverse cities in the world, Dinkins exercised a style of leadership that stressed sensitivity to people from different cultures, lifestyles, and backgrounds. During his time as mayor, Dinkins utilized coalition building as an effective means of addressing the city's many problems.

Born in Trenton, New Jersey, Dinkins was raised by his father after his parents separated when he was six years old. He moved to Harlem as a child but later returned to Trenton, where he attended high school and graduated in the top 10 percent of his class. He joined the U.S. Marines in 1945, after being turned away when he first tried to enlist because that stations' quota for recruiting Negroes had been reached. Following his military career, he enrolled at Howard University, where he graduated *cum laude* with a degree in mathematics in 1950. He earned a law degree from Brooklyn Law School in 1956.

In Harlem, Dinkins became a member of an influential group of African-American politicians that included Denny Ferrell, Percy Sutton, and Charles Rangel. He began his political career when he was elected to the New York State Assembly in 1966, representing the Seventy-Eighth District. He held several positions in city government beginning in 1972 before being elected Manhattan borough president in 1985, on his third run.

In 1989, Dinkins defeated incumbent New York City mayor Ed Koch, who had served three terms in office, to become the first African American elected to head the country's largest city. As mayor, Dinkins quickly moved to address the challenges that plagued New York City. During his time in office, he lowered the crime rate and took steps to revitalize Times Square and other commercial zones. Under his leadership, major urban renewal projects were started in some of the poorer areas of the city. He also established programs that greatly reduced the homeless population.

After one term in office, Dinkins lost his bid for reelection by a slim margin. Although he has not returned to elected office, he has remained active, teaching public affairs at Columbia University's School of International and Public Affairs. He has also been very generous in mentoring and supporting the next generation of political leaders.

FRANKLIN, SHIRLEY CLARK

MAYOR OF ATLANTA, GEORGIA

1945

"I proudly represent all the women who have worked in the fields, toiled in the kitchen, fought for our rights, and challenged our society."

Shirley Franklin is a trailblazer in American politics. She was Atlanta's first female mayor and the first African-American woman elected to head a southern city. Her success is an example of the strides women have made in politics.

A native of Philadelphia, Franklin attended an all-girls high school where she was encouraged to believe that she could do or be anything that she wanted. As a young girl, she wanted to be dancer. But when she was a student at Howard University in Washington, D.C., she became active in the Civil Rights Movement. She earned a bachelor's degree in sociology at Howard University (1968), and earned a master's degree in sociology from the University of Pennsylvania (1969). After teaching political science at Talladega College in Alabama for nearly a decade, in 1978, she was appointed by Mayor Maynard Jackson to the post of commissioner of cultural affairs for the city of Atlanta. When Jackson was succeeded by Andrew Young, Franklin was named chief administrative officer and city manager. Franklin gained notoriety as one of the officials who helped bring the Olympic Games to Atlanta in 1992.

In 1996, Franklin decided to run for mayor. It was her first attempt to seek a political office. Franklin received just over 50 percent of the vote, enough to give her a victory that etched her name in political history. In 2005, she was elected to a second term in office. That same year, she received the prestigious Profile in Courage Award presented by the John F. Kennedy Library Foundation recognizing her management of the city of Atlanta during the critical period of enormous deficit and loss of public confidence in government, a crisis she inherited from her predecessor.

Atlanta mayors can only serve two terms in office. So Franklin was prohibited from running again. Still active, she is currently the chairperson of the board and CEO of Purpose Built Communities and the Barbara Jordan Visiting Professor in Ethics and Political Values in the LBJ School of Public Affairs at the University of Texas at Austin.

JACKSON, JR., MAYNARD HOLBROOK

MAYOR OF ATLANTA, GEORGIA

1938–2003

"Politics is not perfect, but it's the best available nonviolent means of changing how we live."

Maynard Jackson was the first African American to serve as mayor of Atlanta. He was first elected in 1974 when he was only 35 years old. He was elected to a second term in 1978, and in 1990, after being out of office for 8 years, he was elected to a third term. He is the only Atlanta mayor to be elected to three terms in that office.

Jackson was born in Dallas, Texas, the third of six children. His mother Irene, a graduate of Spelman College, had earned a doctorate degree in France and returned to her alma mater as a professor of French. His father, Maynard, Sr., who died when Jackson was 15, was a Baptist minister. Jackson's maternal grandfather, John Wesley Dobbs, was a prominent political and civil rights leader in Atlanta. His family stressed the importance of education and political activism, and Jackson took those values seriously.

After high school, he attended Morehouse College where he received a bachelor's degree in 1956, and subsequently earned a law degree from North Carolina Central University Law School in 1964. He worked as an attorney for the National Labor Relations Board. In 1968, when he was just 30 years old, he ran for a U.S. Senate from the state of Georgia but lost. The following year, he was elected vice mayor of Atlanta. That he was elected mayor in 1973 came as no surprise to those who were paying close attention. In just five years, Jackson had become one of the leading and most influential politicians in Atlanta.

As mayor, he led several huge public works projects in Atlanta, including the construction of what is now one of the world's busiest airports, the Hartsfield-Jackson Atlanta International Airport (which includes the Maynard H. Jackson, Jr., International Terminal). He also oversaw the first development and construction phase of the city's rapid transit rail system. Perhaps his most notable achievement, however, was bringing the 1996 Summer Olympic Games to Atlanta.

After leaving office in 1994, Jackson formed a securities firm that earned him millions of dollars. He also remained active in the Democratic Party as an advocate for grassroots issues until his death in 2003.

Jackson blazed a trail in Atlanta's political history. The city has elected four more African-American mayors since his tenure: civil rights veteran, Andrew Young; Shirley Franklin, Bill Campbell, and Kasim Reed.

NUTTER, MICHAEL ANTHONY

MAYOR OF PHILADELPHIA, PENNSYLVANIA

1957

"Heart, determination, commitment."

Michael Nutter served as the mayor of Philadelphia, America's fifth-largest city, for two terms. The third African American to hold the office, he was sworn in as the chief executive officer in 2008, and remained in that position until 2016.

Born in West Philadelphia, Nutter and his sister were raised by their mother and father who stressed fair play, hard work, and discipline. He attended St. Joseph's Preparatory High School, and worked at a local pharmacy near his home. After graduating from the Wharton School at the University of Pennsylvania in 1979, he worked at the Xerox Corporation, then at the minority-owned investment firm Pryor, Counts & Co.

Nutter's political career began in 1983 with a position working for Philadelphia City Councilman John Anderson. In 1987, he ran for political office himself, losing in a close race for a seat on the Philadelphia City Council. In 1991, he was successful in his bid and served on the city council until 2006. He was also chair of the Pennsylvania Convention Center Advisory Board from 2003 until 2007.

In 2007, Nutter ran for mayor of Philadelphia. He resigned from the city council, and later from his position as chair of the Pennsylvania Convention Center Authority Board, so he could focus on his campaign. He won the Democratic primary in May 2007, and in November of that year, he won in the general election, becoming the third African American to serve as mayor of Philadelphia.

"I had a lot of doubts about whether I could be elected, and people told me it wouldn't happen," he said. "But I had already had a pretty successful career in the city council, so I knew that the time was right for me."

"We're all in this together," Nutter once said. "I learned that lesson growing up in West Philly. When I shoveled the sidewalk, my parents didn't let me stop with our house. They told me to keep shoveling all the way to the corner. I had a responsibility to my community." And that was the way he tried to govern the city of Philadelphia.

Nutter's term as mayor ended in January 2016. He is currently a commentator for CNN, a professor of professional practices and urban policy at Columbia University, and serves on the Homeland Security Advisory Council. He is also a fellow at the University of Chicago Institute of Politics and is a senior fellow at What Works Cities, a data-driven program funded by former New York City mayor Michael Bloomberg.

RAWLINGS-BLAKE, STEPHANIE

MAYOR OF BALTIMORE

1970

"I'm not afraid to tackle big issues."

From an early age, Stephanie Rawlings-Blake has been making a difference with her words and actions. As a child, she often joined her parents in canvassing their neighborhoods in support of social causes.

"I remember standing in front of the supermarket when I was in the first or second grade trying very hard to get the message right," she said. "I got hooked real early and really enjoyed the social aspect and learning that came with being a part of a political campaign."

A curious student, Rawlings-Blake was a hard worker and relentless in her desire to better herself. After graduating from Western High School in Baltimore, she entered Oberlin College in 1988 where she majored in political science. Following graduation, she attended law school at the University of Maryland. She began her political career by running successfully for a seat on the Baltimore City Council.

"I decided to run during my last year in law school because I felt like it was time to pursue my dream in public service," she said. "While my classmates were prepping for exams, I was also prepping for my first run. I felt like it was a doable achievement, and I knew that I was committed and ready."

Rawlings-Blake's election in 1995 made her the youngest person ever elected to the Baltimore City Council. In her new role, she worked hard to make a difference in the city of Baltimore. In 2007, she was selected to serve as city council president. Three years later, when the presiding mayor resigned, Rawlings-Blake assumed the office. Under the Baltimore City Charter, whenever the mayor's office becomes vacant, the sitting city council president automatically ascends to the post for the balance of the term.

"It was a real surprise, but I was ready. My time on the city council gave me great preparation for my job as mayor. I knew what the city needed, and I had plenty of ideas about how to use my skills to improve the quality of life for my constituents."

Elected in her own right as mayor in 2011, Rawlings-Blake earned the confidence of Baltimore residents. During an uprising in 2015 following the death of a Black teen that drew national attention, her leadership helped to establish order in the city. Her term as mayor ended in December 2016.

"I've benefited from having a very clear understanding of who I am and knowing where I've wanted to go," she says. "I feel a real sense of duty to give my very best to the residents of Baltimore and create a legacy that will benefit this city for many generations to come."

REED, MOHAMMAD KASIM

MAYOR OF ATLANTA, GEORGIA

1969

"It's important to be results oriented."

As a child growing up in Atlanta, Kasim Reed knew that he wanted to be a leader. He was an outgoing kid who always demonstrated the ambition and confidence required to do great things.

Reed was born in Plainfield, New Jersey, but his family moved to Fulton County, Georgia, when he was an infant. In school, Reed was a good student who was popular with his classmates and teachers. Goal and results oriented, at the age of 16, he started a jewelry business that by 1989 had earned him $40,000. He enrolled in Howard University, graduating with a degree in political science in 1991. He served on the Board of Trustees as an undergraduate and would go on to become the first person to serve in that capacity as both an undergraduate and an alumnus.

Reed took an internship position with U.S. Representative Patrick Kennedy II after receiving a law degree from the Howard University School of Law in 1995, he worked for Georgia Congressman and civil rights activist John Lewis. Later he joined the law firm of Paul, Hastings, Janofsky & Walker LLP, then became a partner at Holland & Knight LLP, an international law firm with offices in Atlanta.

Not yet 30 years old, Reed was elected to the Georgia House of Representatives where he served from 1998 to 2002. In 2003, he was elected to a seat in the Georgia State Senate and represented the Thirty-Fifth District from 2003 to 2009.

In 2001, when Shirley Franklin decided to run for mayor of Atlanta, her first run for public office, she chose Kasim Reed as her campaign manager. Franklin served two terms (2002–2010) in office.

Because Atlanta has a two-term limit, Franklin could not run again. Reed campaigned successfully to succeed her, assuming office as the city's 59th mayor in 2010. He was elected to a second term in 2014.

As mayor of Atlanta, Reed has made good on his promise to reopen all of the city's recreation centers as safe havens for young people. He has also improved the city's public services, balanced the budget, and bridged racial divides. His administration has made major investments in the city's transportation system and in green technologies.

"Here's the deal ladies and gentlemen, we're a city that gets back up and that thrives," Reed said during his 2014 victory speech. "And what I want to leave you with today and what I hope that you will keep in your hearts is a quote that moves me very much. It says that when we get down, we should remember the words of the author who says he encourages us to be better and to remind us always that when we fall down, to get back up, because the ground is no place for a champion, and that is what we all are."

STOKES, CARL

MAYOR OF CLEVELAND, OHIO

1927–1996

"When you realize that people think that you're going to be some sort of savior from their dilemma, it's very sobering because it imposes a great responsibility upon you."

As the first Black mayor of Cleveland, Ohio, Carl Stokes was a symbol of a changing America. When he was elected in 1967, the Civil Rights Movement had made major gains in securing some legal rights for African Americans. But racial tensions were high. During the 1960s, major cities, including Cleveland in 1966, were hit with uprisings.

With Whites in Cleveland accounting for two-thirds of the city's population, Stokes's election as mayor seemed unlikely. But he was able to build a multiracial coalition that brought the city together, making Cleveland an example that other cities in America would soon follow.

Stokes was born in Cleveland. His father, Charles Stokes, was a laundryman. He died when Carl was just three years old leaving his wife, Louise Stokes, to raise Carl and his brother Louis in Cleveland's first federally funded housing project for the poor. Stokes dropped out of high school in 1944, and after working for a short time, he joined the U.S. Army. He returned to Cleveland after being discharged and earned his high school diploma in 1947. He earned a bachelor's degree from the University of Minnesota (1954) and a law degree from the Cleveland-Marshall College of Law at Cleveland State University in 1956.

After passing the Ohio Bar in 1957, Stokes served as an assistant prosecuting attorney for Cuyahoga County. In 1962, he joined his brother, Louis, who would go on to serve as a U.S. Representative for 30 years, in establishing the law firm Stokes, Stokes, Character, and Terry. That same year, Stokes was elected to the Ohio House of Representatives, where eventually he served three terms. He was the first African-American member of the Democratic Party elected to the Ohio House.

Stokes narrowly lost a bid for mayor of Cleveland in 1965. Two years later, he was successful, drawing national attention as the first Black mayor of one of the 10 largest cities in the United States.

After serving two terms in office, Stokes left Cleveland for New York City where he became that city's first Black television anchorperson. Eight years later, he moved back to his hometown of Cleveland to work as a lobby lawyer. From 1983 to 1984, he was a municipal court judge. President Clinton appointed him ambassador to the Seychelles, a string of islands off the coast of Africa. It was during his time in this office that Stokes died of cancer in 1998. Stokes and his brother, Louis, symbolize the growing acceptance of African Americans in politics and increased African-American political prestige during the 1960s and 1970s.

TAYLOR, IVY

MAYOR OF SAN ANTONIO, TEXAS

1970

"I'm an urban planner who is very interested in inner-city redevelopment and, at the end of the day, creating ladders of opportunity, especially for disadvantaged individuals."

Ivy Taylor made history when she became the first African-American mayor of San Antonio, Texas. In 2014, the San Antonio City Council selected her to complete the term of Julián Castro, who was named by President Barack Obama to serve as the U.S. Secretary of Housing and Urban Development. A year later, Taylor was elected to a full term. She is the first female African-American mayor of a city with a population over 1 million.

Born in Brooklyn, New York, Taylor's parents divorced when she was young. An excellent student, Taylor attended Yale University, where she received a bachelor's degree in American Studies in 1992. She earned a master's degree in urban planning from the University of North Carolina at Chapel Hill in 1998.

During graduate school, Taylor accepted a 10-week internship with an affordable housing organization in San Antonio. In 1999, she returned to San Antonio and began working as the municipal community development coordinator in the Housing and Community Development Department. In 2004, she secured a position with Merced Housing Texas, an affordable housing agency. She was also a member of the City Planning Commission from 2006 to 2008.

"So then I started thinking more broadly, from a public policy perspective, of what else I could do as an individual to help change outcomes for more people, and that's when some community members suggested that I run for city council, which I thought was absolutely bonkers at first," Taylor recalled. "But then, I said, maybe, given the experience that I've had, I can bring that to the table, being a policy maker."

Taylor was right. She was elected to the San Antonio City Council in 2009, and reelected in 2011 and 2013.

As mayor, Taylor has focused on making San Antonio a globally competitive city where all residents are connected to opportunities for prosperity. To achieve this, some of her initiatives have included developing a sustainable city budget, implementing the San Antonio Comprehensive Master Plan, creating a job-friendly environment, growing the workforce, investing in human capital, establishing affordable and livable communities, and building and maintaining basic infrastructure. Registered as a Democrat, she is an independent politician who describes herself as both "fiscally conservative and socially conservative."

TYLER, OLLIE MAE SPEARMAN

MAYOR OF SHREVEPORT, LOUISIANA

1945

"Your vote was your voice, and you sent a message to the next generations that we are vested in the challenges we face to create unity around a vision that will move us to build a stronger, better community."

The ability to push past adversity is an important leadership tool. It's how a leader transforms negative into positive, and faces obstacles and barriers and overcomes them. That's what Shreveport Mayor Ollie Tyler has done. She has overcome a difficult childhood and an abusive first marriage to make major contributions to her community and to her city. She has spent her life working to improve education and create opportunities that make a difference in the lives of others.

The seventh of nine children, Tyler was born on a dairy farm in Blanchard, Louisiana, northwest of Shreveport. She picked cotton as a girl and ironed and cleaned a residence to earn her lunch money. She graduated as valedictorian from her high school and received a National Merit Scholarship to Grambling State University where she received a bachelor of science degree. Later, she received a master's degree in education from Louisiana State University.

Tyler was an educator for more than four decades, and was the first woman and first African American to serve as the superintendent of schools for the Caddo Parish Public School System, a district of 44,000 students. She also served as Louisiana's deputy superintendent of education, and acting state superintendent of education.

During her race for mayor, a piece of Tyler's past resurfaced when it was revealed that she fatally shot her abusive husband in 1968. She was never indicted, and the killing was ruled an "accidental and justifiable homicide."

Tyler overcame this difficult chapter in her life. On December 27, 2014, she reached a milestone, becoming the first African-American woman elected mayor of Shreveport. Among Tyler's goals as mayor are creating a safe environment by providing more police presence in crime-ridden neighborhoods, stabilizing finances by developing an aggressive budget that ensures fiscal sustainability, addressing the city's ailing infrastructure, and establishing partnerships with key stakeholders to expand economic opportunities and attract Fortune 500 companies.

"I will work with a sense of urgency to bring pride, excitement, and economic growth to our city," the new mayor promised her constituency.

YOUNG, COLEMAN

MAYOR OF DETROIT, MICHIGAN

1918–1997

"You can't look forward and backward at the same time."

A s one of the first African-American big-city mayors in the United States, Coleman Young presided over Detroit for 20 years. His rise to the chief executive office came as a result of the gains of the Civil Rights Movement of the 1950s and 1960s.

Born in Tuscaloosa, Alabama, Young was the first of five children. In 1923, his family moved to Detroit hoping to escape the violence and racism that African Americans were forced to endure in the South. But Young soon learned that racism wasn't confined to the South. He remembered an incident when he tried to enroll at De La Salle Collegiate High School in Detroit. "A brother in the order asked if I was Hawaiian. I told him, 'No, Brother, I'm colored.' He tore up the application form right in front of my nose. I'll never forget it. It was my first real jolt about what it means to be Black. That was the end of me and the Catholic Church."

Young finished at the top of his class at Eastern High School in 1935, and he was eligible for a college scholarship. But he wasn't offered enough financial support to cover the cost. So instead of going to college, he took a job with the Ford Motor Company, which later blacklisted him for involvement in union and civil rights activities. He went on to work for the U.S. Postal Service, where he and his brother George started the Postal Workers Union. During World War II, Young was a bombardier with the famous Tuskegee Airmen, serving from 1942 until 1946. He had nearly completed his service when he was arrested for attempting to desegregate an officers' club in Indiana.

After the war, Young returned to Detroit where he continued his union organizing and activism. He was associated with a number of progressive and radical organizations, including the Progressive Party and the United Auto Workers, and was one of the founders of the National Negro Labor Council. During this period of the 1940s and 1950s, Young built a political base on the east side of Detroit. He first ran for office in 1959, losing a bid to become a state representative. In 1960, he was elected as a delegate to help draft a new state constitution for Michigan, and in 1963, he won election to the Michigan State Senate. In 1968, he became the first African American to serve on the Democratic National Committee (DNC). He would go on to become vice chairperson of the DNC.

In 1973, Young set his sights on becoming mayor of Detroit, winning in a close, contested election. He would be elected mayor for an unprecedented five terms, and serve a total of 20 years. During his tenure, Young lowered Detroit's crime rates, helped revitalize the city's economy, initiated construction projects such as the $350 million Renaissance Center business and retail complex, and helped develop the financing package for the Charles H. Wright Museum of African-American History. The Detroit City Airport was renamed the Coleman A. Young International Airport in his honor.

Timeline of African-American Firsts in Politics

1836 Alexander Lucius Twilight is the first African American elected to a state senate (Vermont).

1855 John Mercer Langston is the first African American elected to office in a local U.S. municipality when he becomes town clerk of the Brownhelm Township in Ohio.

1868 Oscar Dunn is the first African American elected as a lieutenant governor (Louisiana).

1868 Pierre Caliste Landry is the first African American elected as the mayor of any U.S. city (Donaldsonville, Louisiana).

1870 Hiram Revels is the first African American elected to either chamber of the U.S. Congress (representing the state of Mississippi in the Senate).

1870 Joseph Rainey is the first African American elected to the U.S. House of Representatives (representing the state of South Carolina).

1928 Oscar Stanton De Priest of Illinois is the first African American elected to the U.S. House of Representatives from a state outside the South.

1934 Arthur W. Mitchell of Illinois is the first African-American Democrat elected to the U.S. House of Representatives.

1952 Cora Brown is the first African-American woman elected to serve in a state senate (Michigan).

1966 Edward Brooke of Massachusetts is the first African American elected to the U.S. Senate, by popular vote.

1966 Robert Clayton Henry of Springfield, Ohio, is the first African American elected as mayor of a U.S. city.

1967 Carl B. Stokes is the first African American elected as mayor of a large U.S. city (Cleveland, Ohio).

1967 Richard Hatcher elected as the first Black mayor of Gary, Indiana.

1968 Shirley Chisholm of New York is the first African-American woman elected to the U.S. House of Representatives.

1973 Tom Bradley is the first African American elected as mayor of Los Angeles, California.

1973 Doris A. Davis is the first African-American woman elected as mayor of a U.S. city (Compton, California).

1974 Maynard Jackson is the first African American elected as mayor of Atlanta, Georgia.

1974	Coleman Young is the first African American elected as mayor of Detroit, Michigan.
1975	Walter Washington is the first African American elected as mayor of Washington, D.C.
1983	Harold Washington is the first African American elected as mayor of Chicago, Illinois.
1989	David Dinkins is the first African American elected as mayor of New York City.
1990	Lawrence Douglas Wilder is the first African American elected as governor of Virginia and the first African American elected governor of any state since Reconstruction.
1991	Sharon Pratt Dixon Kelly is the first African-American woman elected as mayor of a major U.S. city (Washington, D.C.).
1992	Carol Moseley Braun of Illinois is the first African-American woman elected to the U.S. Senate.
1996	Willie Brown, Jr., is the first African American elected as mayor of San Francisco, California.
1998	Lee Brown is the first African American elected as mayor of Houston, Texas.
2007	Deval Patrick is the first African American elected governor of Massachusetts.
2008	Barack Hussein Obama is the first African American to be nominated as a major-party U.S. presidential candidate.
2008	David Paterson is the first African American to serve as governor of New York state.
2009	Barack Hussein Obama is the first African American inaugurated president of the United States.
2009	The U.S. Senate confirms Eric H. Holder Jr. as Attorney General of the United States. He is the first African American to serve in the post.
2013	Cory Booker becomes the first African American elected U.S. Senator from New Jersey. He formerly served as mayor of Newark, the state's largest city.
2013	South Carolina Governor Nikki Haley announces that she has chosen Timothy Scott to replace retiring U.S. Senator Jim DeMint. Scott becomes the first African American to serve as a U.S. Senator.
2016	Kamala Harris is elected as U.S. Senator from the state of California, becoming the first African American and Indian American to serve in that position.
2016	Lisa Blunt Rochester becomes the first African American to win a seat in the U.S. House of Representative from the state of Delaware.
2017	Jewell Jones, a 21-year-old college student, becomes the youngest member to serve in the Michigan House of Representatives.

Political Terms to Remember

act—A written ordinance of Congress, or another legislative body; a statute

affirmative action—Laws mandating increased numbers of women and minorities, especially in employment.

amendment—An alteration of, or addition to a bill, constitution, or some other legal document.

appointment—The act of putting a person into an unelected position, sometimes by approval of another group or body.

assembly—A group of people who are elected to make decisions or laws for a particular country, area, or organization.

bill—A form or draft of a proposed statute presented to a legislature.

campaign—A race between candidates for elective office.

campaign manager—A person in charge of a political campaign.

candidate—A politician who is running for public office.

civil rights—The rights to personal liberty established by the Thirteenth and Fourteenth Amendments to the U.S. Constitution and certain congressional acts.

committee—A special group delegated to consider some matter.

Democrat—A member of the Democratic political party, a party that believes in equality for all people and ruling by the majority and emphasizes that the government is obliged to help create, when necessary, the conditions in which people can achieve and progress. The Democratic Party also believes government must protect the rights of all people.

district—A region marked off for administrative or other purposes.

elected official—Someone chosen by voting to assume an office.

election—The act or process of choosing someone for a public office by voting.

ethics—Philosophical motivation based on ideas of right and wrong.

executive branch—One of the three branches of the U.S. government, comprising the president and all the individuals, agencies, and departments that report to the president, which is responsible for administering and enforcing the laws passed by Congress.

government—The system by which a community or other political unit is governed.

governor—The elected executive head of a state of the United States.

incumbent—An elected official who currently holds an office.

intern—An advanced student or graduate in politics gaining supervised practical experience.

judicial branch—One of the three branches of government charged with the interpretation of laws and the administration of justice. It comprises the U.S. Supreme Court and lower courts.

law—A rule or body of rules of conduct that are natural in human nature or essential to or binding upon human society.

legal—Relating to or characteristic of the official or accepted rules of law.

legislative branch—One of the three branches of U.S. government. It is vested with law-making powers and can formulate and rescind laws. It comprises the House of Representatives and the Senate.

legislature—A group of people who make, amend, or repeal laws.

lieutenant governor—An elected official serving as deputy to the governor of a state of the United States.

mayor—The head of a city or municipal government.

nominate—The act of selecting a candidate for a political office.

nominee—A politician who is running for public office.

oath—A solemn promise, usually invoking a divine witness, regarding future acts or behavior.

policy—A line of argument rationalizing the course of action of a government.

political platform—A document stating the aims and principles of a political party.

politics—The profession devoted to governing and to political affairs.

reform—A campaign aimed at correcting abuse or malpractice in government.

Republican—A major political party in the United States whose core beliefs include smaller government, less domestic governmental spending, strong national security and a larger role for military actions internationally, free trade and capitalism, pro-life and conservative religious values.

resign—To give up or retire from a position.

rule—A principle or condition that customarily governs behavior.

state government—The government of a state in the United States.

state senator—A member of a state senate.

term—A specified period of time in office.

U.S. Congress—The national legislative body of the United States consisting of the Senate and the House of Representatives.

U.S. Constitution—The fundamental law of the United States framed in 1787 by the Constitutional Convention and carried into effect March 4, 1789.

U.S. House of Representatives—The lower legislative house of the U.S. Congress. Membership is determined by population.

U.S. Senate—The upper legislative house of the U.S. Congress. Each state has 2 senators, for a total of 100 in the United States.

vote—The legal expression of one's preference for a candidate or for a measure or resolution.

Index

About the Author

A veteran journalist and bestselling author, Gil L. Robertson IV has edited three anthologies, *Where Did Our Love Go: Love and Relationships in the African-American Community* (2013), *Family Affair: What It Means to Be African American Today* (2008), a "Pick of the Week" selection by *Publisher's Weekly*, and *Not in My Family: AIDS in the African-American Community* (2006).

An entertainment journalist, his work has appeared in publications such as the *Los Angeles Times*, *Atlanta Journal-Constitution*, *Billboard*, *Fortune*, *Essence*, and *Ebony* magazines. He is the co-founder and president of the African-American Film Critics Association (AAFCA), an organization of Black film critics that produces the AAFCA Awards held in Hollywood each spring. *Book of Black Heroes: Political Leaders Past and Present* is his first book for young readers. Visit Gil L. Robertson IV at www.robertsontreatment.com.

Photography Sources

Photographs of the political leaders featured in this book were secured primarily from a variety of governmental and educational sources and are in the public domain. Each photo is identified below by its page number followed by the source.

2, www.whitehouse.gov

6, https://twitter.com/NYGovPaterson55

7, https://chicagopatf.org/about/task-force-members/

8, Library of Congress Prints and Photographs Division

9, http://www.myajc.com/news/local-education/ajc-sepia-greek-spotlight-the-men-omega-psi-phi/ GexOzJEojkUTql3zacn8XP/#PrelcpC_RDG-MjxhBlaq0w

12, http://www.cnn.com/2015/09/28/opinions/booker-fair-chance-act/index.html

13, http://www.history.com/topics/black-history/black-history-month/pictures/black-women-politicians/2004-dnc-carol-moseley-braun (taken at the Democratic National Convention, 2004)

14, Courtesy U.S. Senate Historical Office

16, https://pressroom.usc.edu/files/2015/02/Kamala_Harris_Official_Attorney_General_Photo.jpg

17, Library of Congress Prints and Photographs Division

18, https://www.scott.senate.gov

20, Yvonne Braithwaite Burke private collection

21, Courtesy Mount Holyoke Archives & Special Collections

22, https://www.lacyclay.house.gov

23, http://clyburn.house.gov

24, https://tribwgntv.files.wordpress.com/2013/02/cardisscollins.jpg?quality=85&strip=all

25, https://conyers.house.gov/

26, http://cummings.house.gov

27, http://www.dellumsinstitute.org/news/2016/11/15/moving-past-the-2016-election-cycle-a-debrief

28, Library of Congress Prints and Photographs Division

29, https://ellison.house.gov

30, https://fudge.house.gov

31, Courtesy U. S. Senate Historical Office

32, https://lee.house.gov

33, https://jacksonlee.house.gov

34, http://www.johnlewisforcongress.com

35, https://twitter.com/MiaBLove

36, http://www.politico.com/story/2015/05/park-at-your-own-risk-118164

37, https://payne.house.gov

38, Courtesy U.S. Senate Historical Office

39, https://rangel.house.gov

40, http://www.emilyslist.org/candidates/lisa-blunt-rochester

41, Library of Congress Prints and Photographs Division

42, https://twitter.com/maxinewaters

44, http://www.typp.org/marcus_brandon

45, http://www.sfchronicle.com/author/willie-l-brown-jr-/

46, http://www.legis.state.pa.us/cfdocs/legis/home/member_information/senate_bio.cfm?id=152

48, http://www.oac.cdlib.org/view?docId=hb4c6009nh&brand=oac4&doc.view=entire_text

49, https://twitter.com/AjaLBrown

50, https://search.aol.com/aol/image?v_t=webmail-searchbox&page=1&q=David+Dinkins+photo&s_it=searchtabs&oreq=5cf93942870344ae81ce5fd4d12280fb

51, hereandnow.wbur.org

52, http://www.blackenterprise.com/small-business/maynard-jackson-the-ultimate-champion-for-black-business/

53, www.manutter.com

55, www.kasimreed.com

56, private collection

57, Office of the Mayor Ivy Taylor

58, Office of the Mayor Ollie Mae Spearman Tyler

59, digitalcollections.detroitpubliclibrary.org https://digitalcollections.detroitpubliclibrary.org/islandora/object/islandora%3A215079

Cover design by Stephan J. Hudson, 2nd Chapter